A Guide to
Library Research Methods

A Guide to

Library
Research
Methods

Thomas Mann

OXFORD UNIVERSITY PRESS

New York   Oxford

Oxford University Press

Oxford New York Toronto
Delhi Bombay Calcutta Madras Karachi
Petaling Jaya Singapore Hong Kong Tokyo
Nairobi Dar es Salaam Cape Town
Melbourne Auckland
and associated companies in
Berlin Ibadan

Library of Congress Cataloging-in-Publication Data
Mann, Thomas, 1948–
A Guide to Library research methods.
Includes index.
1. Libraries—Handbooks, manuals, etc.
2. Bibliography—Methodology—Handbooks, manuals, etc.
3. Reference books—Bibliography—Handbooks, manuals, etc.
4. Research—Methodology—Handbooks, manuals, etc.
I. Title.
Z710.M23   1987   027'.002'02   87-1565
ISBN 0-19-504943-8
ISBN 0-19-504944-6 (PBK.)

10 9 8 7 6 5

Printed in the United States of America

For
Jack Nabholtz

Preface

Yet another book on how to do research—why?

The answer lies in the nature of the subject. Quite simply, a multitude of options are involved in doing research, and every writer who looks at them will have a different perspective on how they may be categorized and on which elements should be emphasized over others. My own view has been formed partially on the basis of experiences I've had as an academic researcher at the doctoral level, as a private investigator with a detective agency, as a graduate student in library science, as a free-lance researcher, as a reference librarian at two universities, as a specialist in government documents and microforms, as a database searcher, and as a general reference librarian at the largest library in the world. A second forming element derives from my having observed thousands of other researchers at work, which I have had the opportunity to do for many years. What the aggregate of all this has suggested to me is that most researchers unconsciously work within a framework of very limited assumptions about the extent of information that is easily available to them; and, further, most have only very hazy notions of what is the range of *methods* of searching. It strikes me, too, that other writers on the subject who are not librarians tend to overlook some fundamentally important steps and distinctions in describing the research process, and even unconsciously to perpetuate certain harmful notions. And some librarians who have written on the subject have not placed the weight and emphasis on certain matters that scholars and other investigators require; indeed, library guides frequently offer little more than lists of individual printed sources with no overall perspective on methods or techniques or research. And very few writers of any sort give examples of what to do—or of what not to do, which may be the more instructive.

Much of what I've discovered over the last fifteen years I have had to learn "the hard way," and I especially hope to save the reader from some of the more egregious mistakes and omissions I've been guilty of myself at one time or another. Unlike many people whom I've had the occasion to help, I have had the fortunate (although painful) experience of having had such mistakes systematically brought to my attention by the several shifting professional perspectives I've had on the same types of problems. What this has done for me, I think, is to make certain patterns in research behavior more evident, specifically:

- Patterns in the types of questions that people ask, and in how they ask them.
- Patterns in the usually unconscious assumptions they hold about what can be done.
- Patterns in the bad advice they are sometimes given by teachers, employers, and colleagues.
- Patterns in the mistakes and omissions that reduce the efficiency of their research.

Viewed collectively, these patterns tend to suggest the areas in which most people need the most help, and it is on this group of concerns I wish to concentrate. I hope especially to give readers a sense of the principles and rules involved that are applicable in any situation, and not just an annotated bibliography of particular sources. I also hope that, through some of the examples I've come across in my own research projects and in helping others (from which I've sometimes created composite examples for this book), this guide will give readers a sense not only of the strengths of the various approaches but of their limitations as well. And I hope to provide a perspective of how the advantages and disadvantages of the different methods of searching tend to correct and balance each other in the total information system.

This book could not have been written without the help and expertise of many people. I especially want to thank D. W. Schneider and

Fred Peterson, without whom the project would never have been started. Francis Miksa provided a solid grounding in the principles of systematic research, and a number of other colleagues have provided useful advice, information, or criticisms of the manuscript. Among the latter I wish to thank Adele Chwalek, Lucinda Conger, Sally Fleming, Nanette Gibbs, Gary Jensen, Carolyn Lee, Maria Lacqueur, Rodney Phillips, Roberta Scull, Paul Wasserman, and Steve Zink. Linda Sacks, Theresa Rosen, and Eugene Garfield from the Institute for Scientific Information were most helpful; and I am grateful to the H. W. Wilson Company for permission to quote extensively from one of their booklets.

The list of people from whom I have learned much at the Library of Congress would include whole sections of the Library's staff directory. I am particularly indebted to those from whom I received especially useful information, examples, or criticism: Sam Andrusko, Carol Armbruster, Pat Bernard, George Caldwell, Agnes Ferruso, John Feulner, Judy Furash, Ann Gardner, Anne Marie Gwynn, Annette Hale, Victoria Hill, Richard Howard, Anna Keller, Brent Kendrick, Sandy Lawson, Sarah Pritchard, Judith Reid, Bill Reitwiesner, Dave Smith, and Virginia Wood.

While this book assembles the insights of many people, I must emphasize that its shortcomings are attributable only to myself. The opinions, value judgments, and criticisms expressed within it are also my own; they should not be taken to represent the official views or policy of any organization with which I am or have been affiliated.

Washington, D.C.   T. M.
October 1986

Contents

Comparison of databases to corresponding print indexes—Advantages of computer searches—Limitations and disadvantages of computer searches—Online library catalogs—Full-text searches—Alternative methods of doing Boolean combinations: pre-coordinated and post-coordinated—Need to recognize both strengths and limitations of computer searches—Sources for identifying databases

Abbreviations

ARBA	*American Reference Books Annual*
A&HCI	*Arts & Humanities Citation Index*
BRS	Bibliographic Retrieval Services, a commercial company that provides dial-up acess to computer databases
ISI	Institute for Scientific Information, publisher of *Citation* indexes
LC	Library of Congress
LCSH	*Library of Congress Subject Headings*
NTIS	National Technical Information Service
NUC	*National Union Catalog*
OCLC	Online Library Computer Center (maintains database of cataloging records from many libraries)
RLIN	Research Libraries Information Network
SCI	*Science Citation Index*
SDC	System Development Corporation, a commercial company which provides dial-up access to computer databases
SSCI	*Social Sciences Citation Index*
WLN	Western Library Network

A Guide to
Library Research Methods

1

Initial Overviews: Encyclopedias

The best way to start many inquiries is to see if someone has already written an overview that outlines the most important facts on the subject and provides a concise list of recommended readings. And this is precisely the purpose of an encyclopedia article.

Unfortunately, the *abuse* of encyclopedias tends unnecessarily to limit their effectiveness both for the student writing a term paper and for the business executive, professional, or independent learner the individual will become after leaving the classroom. This abuse comes in two forms: (1) in expecting an encyclopedia to be the beginning *and end* of a complex inquiry, and (2) in expecting the general encyclopedias that everybody knows about to provide a level of detail found only in the specialized encyclopedias that very few people know about. When students get inadequate results from general sets, they frequently tend to change their overall assumptions regarding the future use of all encyclopedias.

The first point to be emphasized is that encyclopedias should be regarded as good starting points for nonspecialists who need a basic overview of a subject or a background perspective on it—but that they should not be seen as compendiums of "all knowledge" that will make further specialized research unnecessary. Nor should one expect currency from such sources—it is the newspaper or the journal and not the encyclopedia that one should turn to for current events (a distinction that seems to be lost on many encyclopedia salesmen). Part of the problem people have with the encyclopedias is that schools (even universities) tend to leave students with only hazy notions of what *other* sources lead quickly to the more specialized or current information, and so researchers often don't perceive what should be starting points within a clear context of what lies beyond.

The second point to be emphasized is that a deeper level of the specialized information *is* available in encyclopedias if one knows enough to look beyond the familiar *Britannica, Americana, World Book,* or *Collier's.* There are scores of specialized sets, or sometimes one-volume works, covering particular fields of knowledge—"specialized" in the sense of concentrating on certain subject areas, not in the sense of being written in the jargon of specialists. The whole purpose of any encyclopedia is to provide an orientation to someone who is not already conversant with the subject being discussed. A real expert will usually not need an introductory overview within his or her own field, but may require one for other areas.

Sometimes, however, the expert will need a large overview of recent or technical developments within his own field; but the sources providing these perspectives are not introductory and they are written in a way that assumes the reader already knows the basics. For them, the researcher will turn to review articles, not encyclopedias. The business executive, professional, or independent learner who has left academia will get the most mileage out of encyclopedias by using the specialized sets in conjunction with, or as background for, these review articles (see Chapter 7).

But even researchers still in school will usually get more information from specialized rather than general encyclopedias. People seeking introductory articles in the sciences, for example, will often be better served by the *McGraw-Hill Encyclopedia of Science and Technology* (20 vols.; McGraw-Hill, 1987), which is the standard set in its field, rather than *Britannica, Americana, Collier's,* or *World Book.* Similarly, those in the social sciences will frequently be better off turning to the authoritative *Encyclopedia of the Social Sciences* (15 vols.; Macmillan, 1930–1935) and its successor and supplement, the *International Encyclopedia of the Social Sciences* (18 vols.; Macmillan, 1968–1979). Students in the arts, too, should consult the specialized works in these areas, among them the excellent *Encyclopedia of World Art* (15 vols.; McGraw-Hill, 1959–1968) and the *New Grove*

Dictionary of Music and Musicians. (20 vols.; Macmillan, 1980). (Don't be misled by the term "dictionary"—in library and publishing terminology it refers simply to the alphabetical arrangement of articles without regard to their length, so it is often synonymous with "encyclopedia.")

Among the scores of relatively little-known specialized encyclopedias these titles are especially good; other works that are considered standard in their fields include:

Dictionary of American History (8 vols.; Scribner's, 1976)

Dictionary of American Biography (20 vols.; reprint, 11 vols. and supplements; Scribner's, 1927–   )

Dictionary of National Biography (22 vols. and supplements; Oxford University Press, 1917–   )

Dictionary of Scientific Biography (16 vols.; Scribner's, 1970–1980)

Dictionary of the History of Ideas (5 vols.; Scribner's, 1973–1974)

Dictionary of the Middle Ages (13 vols.; Scribner's, 1983–   )

Encyclopedia of American Religions (2 vols.; McGrath, 1978)

Encyclopedia of Philosophy (8 vols. reprinted in 4; Macmillan, 1967, 1972)

New Catholic Encyclopedia (17 vols.; McGraw-Hill, 1967–1979)

Interpreter's Dictionary of the Bible (4 vols. and supplement; Abingdon, 1962)

Encyclopedia of Education (10 vols.; Macmillan, 1971)

International Encyclopedia of Education (10 vols.; Pergamon, 1985)

International Encyclopedia of Higher Education (10 vols.; Jossey-Bass, 1977)

International Encyclopedia of Psychiatry, Psychology, Psychoanalysis & Neurology (12 vols.; Van Nostrand Reinhold, 1977)

Funk and Wagnalls Standard Dictionary of Folklore, Mythology and Legend (1 vol.; Funk and Wagnalls, 1973)

Encyclopedic Dictionary of Mathematics (2 vols.; MIT Press, 1977)

Grzimek's Animal Life Encyclopedia (13 vols.; Van Nostrand Reinhold, 1972–1975)

Although the above are certainly important, they by no means exhaust the field. Some other representative titles that may suggest the range of available works include:

The Australian Encyclopedia (6 vols.)

Cassell's Encyclopedia of World Literature (3 vols.)

Dictionary of Named Effects and Laws in Chemistry, Physics, and Mathematics

Encyclopaedia Judaica (16 vols.)

Encyclopaedia of Islam

Encyclopaedia of Religion and Ethics (13 vols.)

Encyclopaedic Dictionary of Physics (9 vols. and supplements)

Encyclopedia of Accounting Systems (3 vols.)

Encyclopedia of American Economic History (3 vols.)

Encyclopedia of American Foreign Policy (3 vols.)

Encyclopedia of American Journalism

Encyclopedia of American Political History (3 vols.)

Encyclopedia of Anthropology

Encyclopedia of Banking and Finance

Encyclopedia of Biochemistry

Encyclopedia of Bioethics (4 vols.)

Encyclopedia of Chemistry

Encyclopedia of Computer Science

Encyclopedia of Crafts (3 vols.)

Encyclopedia of Crime and Justice (4 vols.)

Encyclopedia of Earth Sciences (A series of one-volume encyclopedias covering Oceanography, Atmospheric Science and Astrogeology, Geochemistry and Environmental Sciences, and Geomorphology; other volumes are planned)

Encyclopedia of Educational Research (4 vols.)

Encyclopedia of Electronics

Encyclopedia of Engineering Materials and Processes

Encyclopedia of Fluid Mechanics (6 vols.)

Encyclopedia of Food

Encyclopedia of Historic Places (2 vols.)

Encyclopedia of Human Behavior (2 vols.)

Encyclopedia of Jazz in the Seventies (a companion volume to *Encyclopedia of Jazz in the Sixties*)

Encyclopedia of Library and Information Science (36 vols.)

Encyclopedia of Management

Encyclopedia of Microscopy

Encyclopedia of Military History from 3,500 B.C. to the Present

Encyclopedia of Modern Architecture

Encyclopedia of Mystery and Detection
Encyclopedia of Physical Science and Technology (15 vols.)
Encyclopedia of Prehistoric Life
Encyclopedia of Psychology (4 vols.)
Encyclopedia of Religion (16 vols.)
Encyclopedia of Soviet Law
Encyclopedia of Spectroscopy
Encyclopedia of the American Constitution
Encyclopedia of Themes and Subjects in Painting
Encyclopedia of Urban Planning
Encyclopedia of World Literature in the 20th Century (4 vols.)
The Great Soviet Encyclopedia (32 vols.)
Grzimek's Encyclopedia of Evolution
Guide to American Law: Everyman's Legal Encyclopedia (12 vols.)
International Encyclopedia of Statistics
Kodansha Encyclopedia of Japan (9 vols.)
McGraw-Hill Encyclopedia of Energy
Macmillan Encyclopedia of Architects (4 vols.)
Macmillan Illustrated Animal Encyclopedia
A Milton Encyclopedia (9 vols.)
The Modern Encyclopedia of Russian and Soviet History (projected
    40+ vols., in progress)
Standard Encyclopedia of Southern Africa (12 vols.)
Van Nostrand's Scientific Encyclopedia
World Encyclopedia of Peace
World Encyclopedia of Political Systems and Parties (2 vols.)
World Press Encyclopedia
Worldmark Encyclopedia of the Nations (5 vols.)
Worldmark Encyclopedia of the States

Some of the subjects suggested here are covered by other specialized works, too; and then there are encyclopedias for still other subjects as well.

Foreign-language encyclopedias are often overlooked, but they too are very valuable. Often they are the only sources for information on obscure figures who played roles in the history of foreign countries, and their illustrations are sometimes more useful than those in the English-language sets.

If you wish to find out if your own library has an encyclopedia on a special subject, talk to a reference librarian; or use the forms "[Subject heading]—Dictionaries" or "[Subject heading]—Dictionaries and encyclopedias" in the card catalog.

If you want to find out if a specialized encyclopedia exists even if your library doesn't own it, there are various excellent guides to reference books that will give you this information (see Chapter 13). One particularly noteworthy source is Annie M. Brewer's *Dictionaries, Encyclopedias, and Other Word-Related Books* (3 vols., 3rd ed.; Gale Research, 1982). Volume one lists thousands of English-language sources; volume two, multiple languages with English as one language; and volume three, non-English books. Coverage includes 28,000 works published in the years 1966 through 1981, plus all of those in the Main Reading Room of the Library of Congress regardless of date.

Another especially useful guide is Kenneth F. Kister's *Best Encyclopedias: A Guide to General and Specialized Encyclopedias* (ORYX, 1986), which provides detailed descriptions of over five hundred works. The *ARBA Guide to Subject Encyclopedias and Dictionaries* (Libraries Unlimited, 1986) is somewhat comparable. Eugene Sheehy's *Guide to Reference Books* (American Library Association, 1986) is also very valuable.

The utility of specialized encyclopedias is often discovered by students writing short papers:

A student looking for a good article on the history of bookbinding found that the *Britannica* and *Americana* articles were too short; but when a librarian referred him to the *Encyclopedia of World Art*, which he had never heard of, he found a more detailed discussion that amply suited his needs.

A researcher seeking orientation on the subject of "U.S. isolationism between the World Wars" found less than a column of material in *Britannica;* about two pages' worth, scattered among four articles, in *Americana;* about a column's worth, over three articles, in *Collier's;* and about the same, over four articles, in *World Book.* In the *Encyclopedia of American Foreign Policy,* however, she found a ten-page article on the whole history and philosophy of "Isolationism," about four pages of which were devoted to the interwar period. In addition, the extensive bibliography at the end of the article was much more specifically on target than those in the other encyclopedias.

A student of theology was interested in finding discussions of twentieth-century scholars on the concept of "the Church as Sacrament." Her main problem was that she could not find a subject heading that matched this topic in either the card catalog or the journal indexes. In turning to the *New Catholic Encyclopedia*, however—which has a vocabulary more tailored to Church-related subjects—she found an article on "Sacrament of the Church" and it had a good-sized bibliography appended.

When you need an article on a particular subject (i.e., something less than a book-length treatment), four possibilities should occur to you:

1. An encyclopedia article (generally written as an overview for nonspecialists).

2. A journal/periodical or newspaper article.

3. A "state-of-the art" review article (generally written as a summary for specialists).

4. An essay in an anthology.

Each of the latter three forms is accessible through sources that will be discussed later. For an encyclopedia article, you should start by assuming that there is a *specialized* encyclopedia covering your area of interest and then look for it.

2

Subject Headings
and the Card Catalog

A card catalog lists a library's book holdings; and, while it also lists
the titles of the various journals in the collections, it does not record
the individual articles that appear within them. (For those you will
need the journal indexes, discussed in Chapters 4–6, 8 and 9.) Each
card will provide you with a call number that will enable you to locate
the desired volume on the shelves.

As a rule, every book held by the library will be represented by
several cards filed at different places. Each of these will present an
essentially identical description of the book; the only difference will
be in the top line, which determines where the card will be filed: one
will be under the name of the author; one will be filed under the title
of the work; and one or more will appear under subject headings assigned to correspond to the contents of the book. Some libraries have
catalogs in which all three types of card (author, title, and subject) are
interfiled in one alphabetical sequence, A–Z; others have divided catalogs, in which author and title cards are interfiled in one alphabet
while subject cards appear in a separate file.

Most searches for a particular author's works are relatively straightforward—you just look under the person's last name. There are several potential problems to be aware of, however. If the surname begins
with *Mc*, as in *McDonald*, the cards are usually filed as though the
prefix were spelled *Mac*. Also, in 1981 a major change in cataloging
rules was adopted by most libraries, and it frequently causes confu-

sion. Under the old rules an author's works would be listed only under the author's real name even though his or her books may appear under a pseudonym; thus, for example, works by Mark Twain would appear in the catalog under "Clemens, Samuel Langhorne" and not under "Twain." Under the new rules, however, the books may be cataloged under whatever name appears on the title page. In some libraries, you may have to search in one place for books cataloged prior to 1981 and in another for those that came after; it is a very expensive operation to go back and recatalog thousands of old entries under the new rules, and so not all libraries are doing it.

Searches for a particular title, too, are usually straightforward—you look under the first word of the title, disregarding the initial articles *A, An,* and *The.* (Thus Hemingway's *A Farewell to Arms* would be found in the *F* section of the file.) One noteworthy exception concerns titles of some journals. Under the old rule, if the *name of the sponsoring organization* appears in the title of the journal, then the work is filed under that name and not under the title; thus, for example, the *Journal of the American Medical Association* would (under the old rule) appear as *American Medical Association. Journal*—i.e., it would *not* appear under "Journal" as the first filing word. (A similar situation obtains for titles beginning with terms like *Bulletin of, Annals of, Proceedings of,* etc., followed by the name of an organization.) Under the new rule, the journal may be cataloged under whatever form appears on the title page. A good rule of thumb is simply to check the second possibility if the first one doesn't work. (And note that it is a very common mistake for researchers to overlook a library's holdings of such titles because they look under *Journal, Bulletin, Proceedings,* etc., rather than under the name of the organization.)

One of the most serious and persistent problems researchers have with card catalogs is that of misinterpreting the filing sequence, because it is customarily word-by-word rather than letter-by-letter filing as many people expect. The difference may be illustrated as follows:

Letter-by-letter filing (not used)

Nazareth
N.E.H.
Newark
New England

New Jersey
Newman, John Henry, Cardinal, 1801–1890
NEWMAN, JOHN HENRY, CARDINAL, 1801–1890
News
New York
N.Y.P.D.

Word-by-word filing (is used)

N.E.H.
N.Y.P.D.
Nazareth
New England
New Jersey
New York
Newark
Newman, John Henry, Cardinal, 1801–1890
NEWMAN, JOHN HENRY, CARDINAL, 1801–1890
News

The basic principle in word-by-word filing is that when you have mul-tiword headings or names you first group together all that have the same first word (and subarrange all of them according to second word, then third, etc.) before moving on to any headings or names with a different first word.

Note that in this illustration the name "Newman, John Henry" in capital and small letters is distinct from the name typed all in capitals. The first is an author heading (representing a work *by* Newman); the second is a subject heading (representing a work *about* Newman). Subject headings are always indicated by either of two signals: (1) the top line of the catalog card being typed in CAPITAL LETTERS; or (2) the top line being typed conventionally, but printed *in red ink.*

Note also that initialisms (such as N.E.H., N.Y.P.D.) are filed as though each letter were a separate word. They will therefore appear at the very beginning of their letter section in the catalog, ahead of the full words. (There are some exceptions; for example, I've seen UNESCO filed both at the beginning of the *U* drawers and in the middle, as though it were a word. If there is any confusion, it's best simply to check both possible places. The important point is to know that there *are* two places to look; ignorance of this regularly causes readers to assume that a library does not own acronym titles when they really are available.)

There may be still other disruptions of a normal alphabetical sequence for the sake of creating logical groupings of cards (e.g., in some libraries all personal names file before all geographic names, which file before titles and subjects). If you get confused about anything, remember that it is the job of the reference librarians to help you.

Aside from erroneously assuming that filing is letter–by–letter, the other most frequent problem people have in looking for books in the catalog is finding the right subject heading for their topic. For example, if a reader wants a book on morality, should she look under "Morality"—or under "Ethics"? Or must she try both? The difference is considerable, since the two are nowhere near each other in the filing sequence. Similarly, if another researcher wants information on sentencing criminals to death, should he look under "Death penalty" or under "Capital punishment"? And how does he know that he's thought up *all* of the right terms? Perhaps he should look under "Execution" or some other synonyms as well. Note that the three terms fall into distinct sections of the alphabet.

Reference librarians frequently run into people who are having problems in this regard—for example, one student became frustrated in looking for material on "Telepathy" because it is not under that heading; nor is it under "Mental telepathy." In a standard library catalog works on this subject are filed under "Thought transference." Another researcher wanted books on "Corporate philanthropy"; before asking for help she hadn't found anything because she was looking under "Philanthropy" rather than under the proper heading, "Corporations—Charitable contributions."

Not only the choice of words but also their order may be confusing—for example, should you look under "Surgical diagnosis" or "Diagnosis, surgical"? Under "Heavy minerals" or "Minerals, heavy?" Under "Fraudulent advertising" or "Advertising, fraudulent"? Inverted forms are not used consistently, so there is much room for perplexity.

There is, however, a systematic way in which you can solve most such problems before you even open a drawer in the catalog. Somewhere near the catalog you should be able to find a two-volume set of books called *Library of Congress Subject Headings (LCSH)*. These books are an alphabetical list of terms that are acceptable to the card catalog; they also include words and phrases that are not used, with cross-references to the ones that are. Thus, if you look up "Morality" you will find a note to *"see* Ethics." Similarly, "Surgical diagnosis," which is not used, will tell you to *see* the acceptable form, "Diagnosis, surgical." "Philanthropy" gives you a cross-reference to "Charities"; this, in turn, refers you to "Corporations—Charitable contributions."

The *LCSH* books will also give you a list of other subject headings related to the one you're interested in, so that you can systematically find out all, or most of, the relevant headings. Thus "Death penalty," which is not used, will tell you to *see* "Capital punishment"; under this term you will find a list of other acceptable headings such as "Crucifixion," "Electrocution," "Executions and executioners," "Garrote," "Guillotine," etc. (Fig. 1). And if you look up each of these in turn, you may find further references to other headings (e.g., "Executions and executioners" will refer you to "Criminal procedure," a term not mentioned under "Capital punishment.")

It is very important to note that the cross-references given to other subject headings are to two types. Those proceeded by *sa* (for *see also*) are of equal or *narrower* scope than the term under which they appear. Thus, in the present example, "Electrocution" is a narrower heading than "Capital punishment." Those terms preceded by a double *x (xx)* are of *broader* scope (e.g., "Punishment" is more general than "Capital punishment"). *Neither the* sa *nor the* xx *terms are subsets of the term under which they appear; they are entirely different headings that must be looked up separately.*

Terms preceded by a single *x* (here, "Death penalty") represent possible headings or synonyms that are *not used* as subject headings in the catalog.

(Note: The Library of Congress has recently announced plans to change its notation in future editions of the *Library of Congress Subject Headings* list. Starting with the 11th edition [scheduled for publication in 1988], *sa* will be changed to *NT,* for *Narrower Term; xx* will be changed to *BT,* for *Broader Term;* and the single *x* will be changed to *UF,* for *Used For.* A new designation, *RT* for *Related Term,* will also be introduced.)

Knowledge of the narrower/broader nature of the cross-reference

Death penalty
   See **Capital punishment**

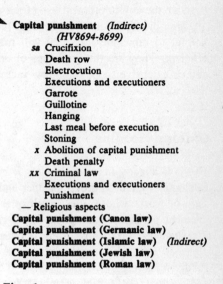

Capital punishment *(Indirect)*
   (HV8694-8699)
   sa Crucifixion
      Death row
      Electrocution
      Executions and executioners
      Garrote
      Guillotine
      Hanging
      Last meal before execution
      Stoning
    x Abolition of capital punishment
      Death penalty
   xx Criminal law
      Executions and executioners
      Punishment
   — Religious aspects
Capital punishment (Canon law)
Capital punishment (Germanic law)
Capital punishment (Islamic law) *(Indirect)*
Capital punishment (Jewish law)
Capital punishment (Roman law)

Fig. 1

structure can help you to expand or refine your search, sometimes through an extended scale of headings, such as the following.

Descending order	*Ascending order*
Chordata	Hamadryas baboon
sa Vertebrates	*xx* Baboons
Vertebrates	Baboons
sa Mammals	*xx* Monkeys
Mammals	Monkeys
sa Primates	*xx* Primates
Primates	Primates
sa Monkeys	*xx* Mammals
Monkeys	Mammals
sa Baboons	*xx* Vertebrates
Baboons	Vertebrates
sa Hamadryas baboon	*xx* Chordata

It is unfortunate, but very few library users—even university professors—are aware of the existence of the *LCSH* books. Nevertheless, they are the key to efficient use of the card catalog.

Three principles used in the construction of the *LCSH* system are helpful to remember, as they will make your searching even more efficient. They are the principles of uniform heading, specific entry, and co-extensive scope of subject indexing.

Uniform Heading

This has already been alluded to. It is the principle that calls for a cataloging system to group together under one subject heading the variety of works whose titles may express that particular idea in many different phrasings and synonyms (e.g., "Death penalty," "Capital punishment") and whose filing is otherwise scattered throughout the alphabet. Further, it requires the same one heading, with appropriate subdivisions (e.g., "—History," "—Law and legislation," "—Study and teaching," "—Bibliography") to group together in one place the many different *aspects* of a subject (e.g., historical, legal, educational, fictional, technical, bibliographical, etc.) whose coverage is otherwise scattered throughout the classification scheme. And in addition it requires that multiple cross-references be established so that a user can *find* the appropriate uniform heading in the first place.

In brief, uniform heading means that catalogers strive to group all materials on the same subject under the same term rather than scatter or repeat them under several synonyms or variant title key words. The advantage is that of the collocation function—you will not have to look in several places for your subject. The potential disadvantage is that you must first be able to discover which synonym is the right one—which you can easily do *if* you know about the *LCSH* books. (By the way, the *sa* cross-references [but not the *xx*] that they provide should also appear on cards filed within the catalog itself; but these are easy to overlook—and they may not appear *at all* in computerized catalogs.) Another less obvious advantage is that if all the books on one subject are listed under only one term, rather than all being listed under each of several headings, then the physical bulk of the card catalog is greatly reduced; it is sometimes the sheer number of cards that makes searching difficult.

Specific Entry

This principle requires a work to be entered under the subject heading that most specifically describes its contents as a whole, rather than under a larger generic or class heading. Thus, if you are looking for material on nightmares, you should not look first under "Dreams" or "Sleep" but under "Nightmares" specifically. Similarly, if you want material on Siamese cats, you should look under the specific heading "Siamese cat" rather than under the generic heading "Cats." One researcher looking for material on Jewish children mistakenly assumed that the proper subject heading would be "Jews"—it isn't; it's "Jewish children," which was in a different drawer. And material under this heading is *not also* listed under the generic heading "Jews." Another reader looking for books on management by objectives wasted a lot of time looking at all the "Management" cards; he should have looked first specifically for "Management by objectives," which is considerably further back in the word-by-word filing. Again, such material will *not* be filed under *both* headings—you have to find the *most specific one* appropriate to the subject. Still another reader interested in the effects of divorce on children made the usual mistake of looking under the generic heading "Divorce" rather than under the specific heading "Children of divorced parents." ("Divorce" in the *LCSH* list provides a *sa* reference to the narrower term.) And—again!—materials listed under the latter heading do not also appear under the broader term because of the principle of uniform heading (i.e., *one* term is chosen). This is not to say that the more general headings may not also be useful, for they may; but you should not *start* with a general heading. The catalog is designed to enable you to find *specific* information, in addition to general; and if you don't look for the narrowest heading you'll probably miss half of what the library has to offer and *all* of the *most* relevant monographs.

The principle of specific entry makes the use of the *LCSH* cross-references essential to an effective search—*you must follow the trail of* sa *or "see also" references* (the ones that lead to *narrower* or *more specific* headings) *until you've reached the heading that most tightly fits your subject*. The point is so important that it bears yet another repetition: remember that these cross-references are *not included in,* and are *not subsets of,* the broader or generic heading under which they appear. (Thus, in Fig. 1, books under "Guillotine" will not be found under the heading "Capital punishment." If you want the former, you must look for that heading directly in the catalog. Note again that in future editions of the *LCSH* list the designation *sa* will be changed to *NT*.)

The two most common and most serious mistakes researchers usually make in using a card catalog are: (1) to assume that the filing sequence is letter-by-letter rather than word-by-word, and (2) to look under the wrong subject terms, which in most cases involves looking under broad or generic terms instead of under specific headings.

Co-extensivity of Headings

As a general rule, works are seldom assigned more than two or three subject headings, for to file cards for each book under a half dozen or more terms would result in a very bulky catalog. (The problem of bulk, by the way, does not arise for catalog records stored in a computer—but more on that later.) The general aim of subject cataloging is to sum up the overall topic of a work in as few subject headings as possible. Thus, a book about "Oranges" and "Grapefruit" will be entered under each of these two terms, because in combination they cover the scope of the whole book. If another book deals with these two topics plus "Tangerines," a third subject heading may be used. However, if a book deals with "Orange," "Grapefruit," "Tangerine," and "Lemon," it will not be cataloged under four different headings. When a work treats four or more related topics, then a *single generic* heading representing all the topics comprehensively will be assigned—in this case, "Citrus fruits." From the card catalog a reader could not tell for sure from this one heading whether the specific topic that interests him—say, "Orange"—is included in the book. Unless the miscellaneous notes on the catalog card list the work's individual chapters—which seldom happens—the reader would simply have to browse through the volume itself. (Note, however, that in originally looking up "Orange" in the *LCSH* list, the user would be informed there, through a double *xx* reference, that "Citrus fruits" is a broader, related heading worth looking at.)

It must be emphasized that the *Library of Congress Subject Headings* system is not fully consistent and that there are many exceptions to all of its general rules. Furthermore, the list of headings in the two-volume set is not an entirely complete roster of all acceptable terms, nor are all of the logical cross-references made between headings (e.g., there is no cross-reference between the related topics "Writing—Identification" and "Forgery"). In particular, most *proper names* of persons, places, and things do not appear in the list, but they can still appear as valid subject headings in the catalog itself.

Thus, although you should always start your catalog searches with the *LCSH* volumes, you must still take the list with a grain of salt. If, after following up its trails of cross-references, you still do not find a subject heading that is suitable, you should simply try the card catalog itself and use whatever terms occur to you. There is always a chance that a book's *title* will correspond to the term you are thinking of. For example, one reader who was looking for material on "famille verte," a color found on some Chinese ceramics, couldn't find a corresponding subject heading in the *LCSH* books; but she did find a relevant book whose title consisted of these words. (And there is then a way to "convert" such a title into a proper *LCSH* term—see below.)

In spite of *LCSH*'s shortcomings, I cannot emphasize too strongly how important it is to be aware that the list exists because, as we'll see later, this same system of vocabulary control is employed wholly or partially by scores of standard indexes, bibliographies, and catalogs other than the card catalog itself. And if you use any source without looking under the right terms you'll miss most of the best material on your subject. For example, one reader looking for material on adolescent suicide checked both the card catalog and the *Social Sciences Index* (for journal articles) but found very little because she was looking under "Adolescent suicide." At that point she asked for help; and, referring to *LCSH*, we found that the proper term is "Youth—Suicidal behavior" at the opposite end of the alphabet. She then went through both sources again using this term and found exactly what she needed.

A further point about *LCSH* is noteworthy if you want to become a supersearcher. There is a slim volume entitled *Library of Congress Subject Headings: A Guide to Subdivision Practice* that is well worth knowing about. (Copies are available for $10 from the Cataloging Distribution Service, Library of Congress, Washington, D.C. 20541.) It provides a list of the standard subdivisions that can be used to qualify the headings in the regular *LCSH* list. Some of the more useful ones are:

[Subject heading]—Bibliography
                —Criticism and interpretation
                —Description and travel—Views
                —Dictionaries and encyclopedias
                —Directories
                —History
                —History—Sources
                —Management
                —Maps
                —Pictorial works
                —Social life and customs
                —Statistics
                —Study and teaching

A working knowledge of these subdivisions will greatly enhance your ability as a researcher, especially since they are often not listed in the *LCSH* books under the terms they apply to. You just have to know in advance that such things exist and that they can be used in a variety of places to qualify terms and make them more specific. There are *hundreds* of such subdivisions, so if you're serious about learning to do research in a *systematic* fashion, you'll have to spend some time browsing through the *Guide*. Success in using these subdivisions depends on your "getting the feel" of which ones you can expect to find. They are frequently not noticed in the catalog itself because of the filing scheme—for example, in one library I worked in the heading "Greece—History" is separated from the unqualified term "Greece" by the interposition of fifteen other subdivisions, such as "Greece—Description and travel" and "Greece—Foreign relations," plus a variety of titles starting with the name of the country. And, because of the principles of uniform heading and specific entry, most of the history books are entered under the subdivided heading and *not* under the general term "Greece" by itself. And so a researcher could easily miss them unless he suspects beforehand that a form such as "Greece—History" should exist.

Similarly, most subjects can be subdivided geographically; thus, for example, you would have to suspect in advance that "Mass media—United States" may be a better heading than "Mass media" alone. At another university library where I worked, the two are separated by over three dozen other subheadings; at the Library of Congress they are in completely separate drawers. The point is that the most relevant works on a topic may very well have a "—United States" subdivision; but you may easily miss the form unless you are deliberately looking for it. The best way to avoid such difficulties is always to browse quickly through *all* subdivisions of a topic, even if it involves skimming through a whole drawer (or more) of cards. It is still worthwhile to study the *Guide,* however, for if you are aware in advance of the possible existence of the standard and geographic subdivisions, you will be more alert in searching for them—which will make a significant difference in the efficiency of your finding them.

The first way to find the right term for your subject is thus to use the *Library of Congresses Subject Headings* list. There is also a second way, however; and this is to use what are called tracings. These are the notations that appear at the bottom of a catalog card—they are a listing of all the headings (including subject headings) under which copies of that card will be filed. Most researchers never even notice them. And yet they are very important because they can frequently provide you with an entry into the subject heading system when you are unsuccessful with the *LCSH* volumes.

For example, a reader who was interested in the student riots in France in the late 1960s was having trouble finding a good subject heading to use. He was already aware of one book on the subject, however: Patrick Seale's *Red Flag/Black Flag: French Revolution, 1968.* The catalog card for this book is reproduced in Figure 2. Note that the tracings indicate that this work has been assigned two subject headings: "Paris—Riot, 1968" and "College students—France—Political activity." This told him that other, similar books would probably be found under these same headings, which proved to be the case.

A second researcher interested in books on the White House found a set of titles when he looked under "White House"; but the tracings for these *titles* informed him that the correct *subject heading* is "Washington, D.C. White House"—and this led him to a set of records many times larger than the first set (Fig. 3). The difference, again, is that cards under the subject heading don't have to have the specific words "White House" in their titles—they can refer to it as "1600 Pennsylvania Avenue," "Home of the Presidents," or "The Executive Mansion." *A subject heading groups together in one place all such variant phrasings that may scatter titles all over the alphabet.*

A good researcher will develop the habit of *always looking at the*

DC412
.S4   **Seale, Patrick.**
1968   Red flag/black flag; French revolution, 1968, by Patrick
             Seale and Maureen McConville. ₁1st American ed.₁ New
             York, Putnam ₁1968₁

                 252 p.   illus., ports.   22 cm. $6.95

➤   1. Paris—Riot, 1968.   2. College students—France—Political ac-
        tivity.   ɪ. McConville, Maureen, joint author.   ɪɪ. Title.

        DC412.S4   1968   944.3′6′083   68–57448

        Library of Congress   ₍5₎

                           Fig. 2

tracings for any book that seems to be relevant for they provide subject headings that may not otherwise be found. *This is a particularly
valuable way to find headings that use standard or geographic subdivisions,* as these qualifiers are often omitted in the *LCSH* list, and they
are easy to miss in the card catalog. For example, one researcher interested in the phonetic peculiarities of the Cockney dialect thought
that he had done a good job in finding the heading "English language—Dialects"; but when he looked up "Cockney" as a title word
he found through the tracings that he should have looked under "English language—Dialects—England—London," which is far separated
from the first heading in the word-by-word filing.

Another way to find subject headings through tracings is by using
the *National Union Catalog (NUC)* and its supplements. This astonishing set is the closest thing to a list of every book that has ever been
published worldwide; for most entries it provides a reproduction of a
full catalog card, including tracings (see Chapter 10). The *NUC* is
arranged by authors' names, so if you already know of one book that's
useful, you can look it up and find the subject headings assigned to it
even if your own library doesn't own the book. For books published
in America since 1876, the various cumulations of the *American Book
Publishing Record* also provide tracings. And, if you already have a

The White House.

F204
.W5L53   Leish, Kenneth W
          The White House, by Kenneth W. Leish and the editors
       of the Newsweek Book Division. New York, Newsweek
       ₁1972₁

            170, ₁1₁ p. illus. (part col.) 30 cm. (Wonders of man)

            Bibliography : p. ₁171₁

➤   1. Washington, D. C. White House. 2. Presidents—United States—
       Biography. 3. Washington, D. C.—Social life and customs.   I.
       Newsweek, Inc. Book Division. II. Title.

       F204.W5L53   917.53   72–178706
       ISBN 0–88225–020–5; 0–88225–021–3 (deluxe ed.)   MARC

       Library of Congress   72 ₁4₁

                              Fig. 3

recent book in hand, you can usually simply look on the reverse side
of the title page for "Cataloging in Publication" data, which will also
give you the tracings for that book.

There are a host of other subtleties and tricks in using the *LCSH*
system that serious researchers may wish to be aware of, such as the
rule of thumb of structuring headings in the areas of the social sciences
according to the form [Place]—[Subject], rather than [Subject]—[Place].
Interested readers should peruse Lois Mai Chan's *Library of Congress
Subject Headings: Principles and Applications* (Libraries Unlimited,
1986), which is the best treatment of the subject. This book is not for
librarians only; it will be valuable to anyone who wishes to learn how
to mine the card catalog with any degree of efficiency.

There are both advantages and disadvantages to developing information through the card catalog. The primary advantage—and it is an
important one—is that anything you find in it is likely to be immediately available to you on the shelves; you needn't go to another library
for the material or use interlibrary loan. (If a book is not on the shelf
where it should be, you should look for a daily computer-updated
printout at either the Reference or Circulation desks. Most libraries
will have one; it will list all books checked out to individuals or placed
on reserve.)

One of the disadvantages, of course, is that the card catalog will list only your own library's collections, which may not contain the best or the most recent books on your particular subject. Further, retrieval is complicated by the standard practice among catalogers of assigning as few subject headings as possible to a work—that is, only as many as summarize its contents as a whole. You cannot therefore tell from the subject headings what the contents of individual sections or chapters are. (This is the difference between subject cataloging and indexing.) With one notable exception, the best way to find out what's in the chapters is to browse the contents of the books themselves, which you can locate in the stacks through their call numbers (see Chapter 3).

The exception involves collections of different essays by one or more authors. For most such works, the individual essays in the volume are each indexed separately in an ongoing publication called *Essay and General Literature Index* (H. W. Wilson, 1900–   ), which provides an author and subject approach. And the subject terms it assigns follow essentially the same list of *Library of Congress Subject Headings* used by the card catalog. This *Index* is very similar to a journal index—the only difference is that the articles it covers are in book anthologies rather than in periodicals. Each issue (semiannual with bound annual and five-year cumulations) contains a list of the anthologies it indexes; there is also a separate cumulative volume of *Works Indexed, 1900–1969*. The *Essay and General Literature Index* is a good supplement to the card catalog, for it provides deeper subject access into many books than the catalog does. And libraries frequently use its lists of works indexed as buying guides for developing their collections.

The *Index* is especially valuable to professors and graduate students because it supplies good access to scholarly *Festschriften*. It is noteworthy for undergraduates, too, because for every ten people who know of the existence of the specialized journal indexes, only one will know of the *E&GLI*. Anyone who uses it is likely to be the only one in the class to have discovered the material it leads to. And, as a wise debater once said, "An expert is someone who can cite a source that nobody else knows about."

The *E&GLI* is not the only index that picks up essays from anthologies (*Religion Two, Historical Abstracts, MLA International Bibliography,* and *Anthropological Literature* are examples of others in specialized fields); but it is the best overall and multidisciplinary source of its type, and its coverage extends much farther back (to 1900) than the others.

The sources I am emphasizing in this book are those that allow access by subject; but there are other indexes analogous to the *E&GLI* that list and index individual items other than essays within anthologies, for example, poems, plays, and short stories. These can be identified through the reference sources discussed in Chapter 13.

The overall points to remember about subject headings are that:

- You *must* find the subject term that is acceptable to the system, which will very often not be the term you think of by yourself.

- One way to find the right term(s) is by following the cross-references in the *Library of Congress Subject Headings* list, which is the standard used by libraries all over the country.

- You must pay particular attention to the *sa* or *see also* cross-references, which lead you to the *most specific* headings. Books are entered *only* under the most specific headings applicable to them and *not also* under larger generic headings. (Note: After 1988 the *sa* designation will be changed to *NT* for *Narrower Term*.)

- A second way to find the right subject headings is to use the tracings at the bottom of any catalog card representing a book you know to be relevant, for these notations will tell you the terms you should look under for similar books.

- You should realize that many other catalogs, indexes, bibliographies, and databases use essentially the same *LCSH* list of terms.

Subject heading searches, however, are only one method of gaining access to information. For the sake of providing a large overview, let me anticipate a few points to be discussed in subsequent chapters and mention here that six alternative methods of searching can be used when no subject heading exists or when you wish to find sources in addition to those turned up under subject headings:

- Systematic browsing (see Chapter 3).
- Key word searches (see Chapters 5 and 9).
- Citation searches (see Chapter 6).

- Searches through published subject bibliographies (see Chapter 8).
- Computer searches (see Chapter 9).
- Talking to knowledgeable people (see Chapter 11).

Each of these approaches—like searching with subject headings—has its own advantages and disadvantages; and, collectively viewed, each has a strength that compensates for a weakness in the others. An awareness of the basic structure of the relationships of only these few distinct methods can have a very large effect in increasing the efficiency of your research.

3

Systematic Browsing and Use of the Classification Scheme

Librarians sometimes meet with resistance when they suggest that if readers want certain information they should browse the library's bookshelves in a particular area. Evidently, some people assume—if it occurs to them at all—that browsing is at best a haphazard and inefficient way to do research.

Just the opposite is true. Systematically browsing the shelves is a very useful method of subject retrieval, and in some cases it is the most efficient method of all. Historically, the practice of shelving books in a classified arrangement (i.e., so that books on the same subject will be placed next to each other in convenient groups) antedates the invention of the card catalog. Indeed, for many decades subject access to research collections was available *only* through the groupings of similar books together on the shelves. The great age for the development of classification schemes was around the turn of the century, when the Library of Congress and Dewey Decimal classifications were devised; few libraries had card catalogs then, so much effort was expended in creating precise categories and subcategories to reveal subtle relationships among subjects.

To understand the immense value of classification schemes it is worthwhile to consider the possible alternative methods of shelving books. A library *could* simply shelve them in the order of their acquisition—catalogers would then have only to assign sequential whole numbers to the books (1, 2, 3, . . .). Such a system would be capable

of storing an infinite number of volumes; and, as long as the number
that appears on the catalog card corresponds to the number on the
book, readers could easily locate any volume on the shelves. The library would save thousands of dollars every year if this scheme were
used, since it would require professional catalogers only for describing
the books and devising subject headings for the card catalog and not
for also creating systematic call numbers. It would save money, too,
in preventing the need for redistribution of books caused by unantici-
pated bulges of growth in particular subject classes; in a whole number
system, the only area that needs room for growth is the very end of
the sequence.

Another possibility is that the library could shelve books strictly
according to their size—all six-inch tall books together, all eleven-inch
tall books together, and so on. If this were done, then the vertical
distance between bookshelves could be adjusted precisely so that there
would be no wasted space above volumes caused by height differen-
tials. Given that there are miles of shelving in any large library, this
would enable storage to be much more space efficient, which would
save a lot of money and allow room for larger collections. Just such a
system, in fact, is used by the Center for Research Libraries in Chicago, which stores hundreds of thousands of little-used volumes that
are available to other libraries through interlibrary loan. The New York
Public Library also uses a system of shelving by height. Conventional
subject groupings do not exist in such collections.

Both of these methods would be much less expensive to hard-pressed
library budgets than the usual practice of maintaining a subject-class
arrangement. So why is the latter still used when cheaper alternatives
are available?

The problem is that the alternative schemes impose a major disadvantage on researchers—namely, that if someone wants a book on any
subject, he or she must know *in advance specifically which book* is
wanted in order to retrieve it from the storage system. There is no
possibility of efficient browsing when the subjects of the books are
irrelevant to their arrangement. In a height system, if one book on
anthropology is six inches tall and another is eight inches they may be
shelved on entirely different floors; or, in a sequential system, if one
book came into the system a year after the other, they may be separated by two hundred feet of cookbooks, car repair manuals, and Gothic
novels.

One of the major advantages of a classified arrangement of materials is that it enables you to find relevant works that you didn't specifically know about in advance. It allows for—indeed, encourages—*discovery by serendipity.* The value of such discovery may be incalculable for any given search. One student in an academic library, for example, had to write a lengthy paper on the poet Shelley. He wasn't sure how to narrow his topic, but he thought that having some biographical information on the poet might help. He found the call number of a biography through the card catalog, but when he got back among the shelves to retrieve it he noticed that right nearby was a copy of Clement Dunbar's *A Bibliography of Shelley Studies 1823–1950* (Garland, 1976). This source presented to him much of the range of studies that had already been done, which gave him a clearer idea of the range of questions he could "allow" himself to ask. The subject-grouping arrangement of the books in the stacks had thus enabled him to recognize a useful source even when he hadn't been looking for it specifically.

The classified arrangement is equally useful for researchers who already have a very clear idea of what information they specifically want to find, but who don't know which source will have it. One reader wanted information on an extremely specific point: he had been told by a questionable source that educated Victorian Londoners would preferably spell *hell* with a capital rather than a small *h,* and he wanted to check the truth of the matter as it related to assessing the educational level of an anonymous letter writer of the period. The *Oxford English Dictionary* was ambiguous on the point, so he went to the sections of the collection that deal with the history of the language and its usage, then systematically browsed the books. He eventually found a style manual for a Victorian London newspaper, which instructed its readers to use the small *h* in *hell;* and this was enough to make him reject what he had been told. He hadn't been looking for a newspaper style manual for that date and place—in fact, it had never occurred to him that such a thing would exist. But in using the classification scheme as it is meant to be used he found it anyway because he had consciously put himself in a position where he could *recognize* a relevant source when he saw it.

In both of these cases the card catalog was not very helpful—in the one, the reader did not have a specific subject in mind; in the other, the researcher's subject was much *too* specific to be picked up by the

co-extensive subject-heading system. The solution to both problems
lay in the readers' browsing the books themselves, not the superficial
cards that represent them. The major advantages of the shelf-scheme
are thus two: (1) it encourages discovery by *recognition* and *serendipity,* and (2) it allows much greater *depth* of access to monographs than
the card catalog does.

The advantages and disadvantages of the card catalog and the book
arrangement scheme are rather neatly complementary—and they are
that way by design. One disadvantage of the card catalog is that it will
tell you only the subject of a book as a whole, and not the contents of
individual sections, paragraphs, or sentences. This problem is corrected by the classified book stacks—any book that you find on the
shelves will immediately present its full contents for your inspection.
You will not have just two or three short subject headings to look at,
but the table of contents, index, preface, full text, and illustrations.

One disadvantage of the shelf scheme is that any book within it can
be shelved at only one call number, even though it may cover many
subjects. This problem is remedied by the card catalog, which provides multiple points of access for each book (i.e., author, title, and
usually two or three subject headings filed at various places in the
catalog). The trade-off here is between the depth of access to a particular work and the number of points of access to it.

Conversely, a single subject may have many different aspects (e.g.,
historical, biographical, social, legal, technical, dramatic, fictional,
philosophical, military, political, educational, economic, artistic, medical, sociological, religious, bibliographical, etc.), and so the in-depth
access that you need may be impeded by the many relevant books
being scattered throughout the classification scheme. For example, in
the Library of Congress system the range of class numbers E51–99
contains a wealth of material on the history and culture of "Indians of
North America." However, books on Indian languages are in PM101-
7356; collections of fictional writings by Indian authors are in PS505
and PS5891; the history of Col. William Crawford's Indian campaign
is in E238; amateur Indian plays are in PN6120.16; Indian laws are in
KF8201-8228; works on hospitals for Indians are in RA981.A35; and
bibliographies on Indians are in Z1209.[1]

Similarly, while material on "Drinking and traffic accidents" has a
home base at HE5620.D7, it also appears in nine different K and KF

legal classes, in seven different RC medical classes, in seven different HV social pathology classes, and in several other areas including AS36, J905.L3, QC100, TL152.3, and Z7164.T81—for a total of *thirty-two different browsing sections*. Anyone who simply scans the HE5620.D7 area may miss at least as much important information as he or she finds. The situation with "Drug abuse" is similar: even if one found the bulk of material contained in several different classes within the HV5800s, one would still be likely to overlook dozens of other areas including AS36 (societies), BV4470 (pastoral theology), several H classes (social sciences) other than HV, several KF classes (U.S. law), LB1044 (teaching), a number of P (fiction) and R (medical) areas, QP37 (human physiology), TX943 (food service) and two different Z classes (bibliographies).

Since at least some such scattering is likely to be found with any subject, how do you identify all the classes into which the topic can fall? Here again the complementary nature of the card catalog comes to the rescue—works that are scattered among many different classes in the book stacks are grouped together under one heading within the card catalog, enabling you to find which classes you should browse. (In the above examples the grouping function is achieved by the three subject headings that appear in quotation marks.) The trade-off here is between the depth of access to particular aspects of a broad subject and the range of access to all of them.

Thus, while the card catalog corrects the weaknesses of the classified stacks (i.e., by providing multiple points of access to works that can have only one position in the classes, and also by grouping under one subject heading works that are scattered among many classes), the shelf-browsing system in turn corrects the defects of the card catalog (by providing in-depth access to full texts, free of the constraints and filters of an artificial vocabulary of subject headings arranged alphabetically rather than logically).

This complementary relationship is underscored by the policy of the Library of Congress in assigning subject headings to topical or documentary films. Since it is virtually impossible to browse a film collection for subject content (i.e., you cannot just pick up a film and flip through it), and since users must therefore rely almost entirely on catalog records for retrieval, LC provides such materials with extra subject headings.[2] Note the underlying assumption held by the librarians that this exception points out: in normal circumstances readers will *not* rely entirely on the catalog for subject access, but will supplement its approach with shelf-browsing.

If you don't use both approaches, in other words, you are not using the library as it is set up to be used—and you are therefore probably missing half of what the library's monographs have to offer on your topic. The most efficient way to do library research is to match your retrieval technique to fit the library's storage technique, for in this way you will be exploiting the *internal structure* of the system. This structure *assumes* that you are aware of the complementary advantages and limitations of the card catalog and book classification systems. You must be cognizant of the trade-offs involved, because the two do not duplicate each other, and if you use only one part and not the other, you are neglecting half of the basic retrieval system.

I emphasize the point because there seems to be a kind of "threshold of awareness" that many readers have to cross regarding the value of browsing in the bookstacks. While most researchers have had, at one time or another, experiences of serendipitous discovery in a library, many of them regard such experiences as more due to luck than to system. But it actually *is* the system that is working in such cases—and if you area aware of this, you can exploit that system *consciously* and *deliberately* rather than haphazardly. You can make your "luck" improve, and do it systematically.

In working on a variety of research projects I have frequently found that browsing the subject groupings of books in the stacks is the *only* way to find the desired information. I was once looking for information on the Civil War ironclad *Barataria*. "Barataria" is not a subject heading in the catalog; the best one I found was "United States— History—Civil War, 1861–1865—Naval operations." The cards in the catalog under this heading led me to the E591–600 stack area; and in browsing through the various books there, paying special attention to tables of contents, chapter headings, and indexes, I found a great deal of specifically relevant material. Similarly, it was systematic browsing in the stacks that turned up information on Abraham Lincoln's pocket knives, an anecdote about James Thurber's mother, and figures on the number of casualties at Guadalcanal. Although all this information lay waiting in the library's books, *none* of it was specifically identifiable through the subject headings in the card catalog.

The importance of the browsing system makes it essential that books actually be on the shelves where they should be so that people can discover them. In this light, it is very detrimental to researchers that some college professors check out large numbers of books and keep them for whole semesters—or even years—in their offices. Subject access to these volumes is significantly diminished, for the material in them cannot always be identified through the card catalog. It is all the more serious a problem because the books that are removed from the system in this way are often the very best works on their subjects. Professors should remember to return *all* books they are not currently using, for simply to say "I'll return it if someone asks for it" is to display a fundamental disregard of the way researchers have to work.

The best way to find which classification number areas to browse is through using the card catalog (i.e., look up the relevant subject headings and note the call number ranges on the cards). A second way is to use the *Library of Congress Subject Headings* list directly. When you look up a heading you will frequently find that it tells you which range of call numbers corresponds to that subject (Fig. 4). The *LCSH* list does not provide numbers for all subjects, however; nor does it give numbers for all aspects of a subject. That's why it's better to use the card catalog.

Using classified arrangements to enable yourself to recognize sources that you weren't specifically looking for has applications beyond the use of the book stacks. Even if the material being arranged in classified order is merely a set of cataloging records for books rather than the works themselves, the classified or logical groupings will still enable you to notice citations that you might overlook in an alphabetical sequence. Some bibliographies are therefore arranged in this manner; one, the annually cumulated *American Book Publishing Record,* is particularly noteworthy. It lists the year's production of American books in subject groupings that shade into each other; it is therefore a good companion to *Subject Guide to Books in Print,* which is arranged alphabetically by LC subject headings. Both sources can alert you to current books that don't happen to be held by your own library (see Chapter 10).

Systematic browsing is especially useful when dealing with primary records. Primary records are those generated by a particular event, by those who participated in the event, or by those who directly witnessed it. Thus, for example, a researcher interested in World War II propaganda would be interested in such primary sources as copies of leaflets

Chlorides *(Biochemistry, QP535.C5;* ◀━━━
        Chemistry, QD181.C5) ◀━━━
    sa Aluminum chloride hexahydrate
       Cisplatin
       Lead chloride
       Lithium chloride
       Tetrachlorides
       Vinyl chloride
       specific chlorides, e.g. Cuprous chloride
  Example under Chemistry, Inorganic
    Physiological effect *(QP913.C5)* ◀━━━
      sa Plants, Effect of chlorides on
    Spectra

Electric power transmission *(Indirect)*
        (TK3001-3521) ◀━━━
    sa Electric lines
       Electric power distribution
    x Electricity—Transmission
       Power transmission, Electric
    xx Electric lines
       Electric power distribution
       Electric power systems
 — Alternating current *(TK3141-3171)* ◀━━━
    xx Electric currents, Alternating
 — Direct current *(TK3111)* ◀━━━
    x Direct current power transmission
    xx Electric currents, Direct
 — Equipment and supplies
    sa Electric power transmission
       equipment industry

      GEOGRAPHIC SUBDIVISIONS

 — New Mexico
    sa Four Corners-Ambrosia-Pajarito 500
      kV Transmission Project
**Electric power transmission equipment
     industry** *(Indirect) (HD9695)* ◀━━━
    xx Electric power transmission—
      Equipment and supplies

Fig. 4

dropped from airplanes, typescript accounts of the flights written by those who planned or flew them, and first-hand accounts of civilians on the ground who found such leaflets. Secondary sources are the later analyses and reports written by nonparticipants, usually in published literature—although a published source can itself be primary if it is written by a participant or a witness or if it directly quotes one. Many collections of primary manuscripts or "raw materials" exist on an incredible array of subjects, and can be identified through the sources discussed in Chapter 10 and in the Appendix. However, such collections are more often than not poorly indexed, or not indexed at all, so researchers usually must simply browse through them. The principle is the same, though: *first put yourself in a situation where the information you want is likely to exist, and then look around so that you can recognize valuable things when you see them.*

One of the major themes of the present book is that a variety of techniques can be used to find information, that each of them has both advantages and disadvantages, and that no one of them can be counted on to do the entire job of in-depth research. What is required is always a mixture of approaches, so that the various trade-offs can balance each other. My observation, however, is that in this age of proliferating indexes, abstracts, catalogs, and databases, the research technique of systematic browsing tends to be overlooked by researchers who are infatuated with the flashier electronic approaches. The fact remains, however, that the vast bulk of humanity's written memory contained in books is not in the indexes and databases in the first place; and researchers who neglect systematic browsing of the texts of books are missing a vast store of material that cannot be efficiently retrieved in any other way.

Notes

1. This example is taken from a useful booklet entitled *The Library of Congress Shelflist,* edited by Linda K. Hamilton (University Microfilms Internationa, 1979).

2. See Lois Mai Chan, *Library of Congress Subject Headings* (Littleton, Colo.: Libraries Unlimited, 1986), p. 223.

4

Subject Headings and Indexes to Journal Articles

We have seen that the card catalog does not provide in-depth subject access to monographs (i.e., at the chapter level or below) because it was designed not to duplicate a means of entry already provided by the shelf-browsing/classification scheme. Similarly, it does not provide access to individual articles within magazines or journals because a suitable alternative avenue exists: special journal indexes. It is not cost effective for a general library's card catalog to duplicate a means of access that is already available elsewhere; moreover, if the catalog did provide author, title, and subject access to each article in every journal in the library, then it would be so bulky that it would take up an entire floor of the building and would be so much more difficult to use that access to monographs would be correspondingly diminished.

Indexes to journals exist in all subject areas. As with encyclopedias, however, most people are aware of only a few general sets (e.g., *Readers' Guide to Periodical Literature*), but would be better served if they used the more specialized ones. The whole point, again, is that the more you are conscious of the range and depth of resources available—beyond the superficial, general sources—the more substantive and probing will be the questions you allow yourself to ask. Most people give up in their research way too soon because they are not aware of the existence of the best sources for their subject.

The most important journal indexes you need to know about for basic library research are known collectively as the Wilson indexes, as they are published by the H. W. Wilson Company of New York, which also publishes the *Essay and General Literature Index*. Each has a similar format, and most of them provide author and subject (but not title) access to individual journal articles. Each also follows the general filing conventions of the card catalog (e.g., word-by-word rather than letter-by-letter alphabetization; the prefix *Mc* filed as though it were spelled *Mac;* all author and subject entries interfiled in one alphabet). Each entry in the indexes provides the title of the article (although the entry itself is not *filed* under the title), the name of the periodical, volume, pages, date, and author; there are also very useful notes that will tell you whether the article includes illustrations, diagrams, or a bibliography. Each index has a separate "Book Review" section, too.[1] The following are ones that you want to be aware of:

Readers' Guide to Periodical Literature (1900–   ).   This is the basic "umbrella" index covering all subject fields. (But see also the *Index to U.S. Government Periodicals* discussed in Chapter 12.) *Readers' Guide* indexes about 180 periodicals, most of which are of the popular "newsstand" type (i.e., the articles usually don't have footnotes), among them *Time, Newsweek, Better Homes and Gardens, Fortune, Good Housekeeping, Popular Photography,* etc. It comes out twice a month, generally, with quarterly and annual cumulations.

Social Sciences Index (1974–   ).   Like *Humanities Index* (below), it is a successor to *International Index* (1907–1965) and *Social Sciences and Humanities Index* (1965–1974). It provides access to about 300 scholarly periodicals in the fields of anthropology, area studies, consumer affairs, human ecology, economics, environmental studies, geography, international relations, law and criminology, nursing, pharmacology, political science, psychiatry, psychology, public administration, public health, social work, sociology, and urban studies. One particularly noteworthy subject heading is "Tests and scales," which will lead you to information on psychological and other tests. It comes out quarterly, with annual cumulations.

Humanities Index (1974–   ).   Successor to two other indexes going back to 1907, this source covers about 300 scholarly journals in the fields of archeology, area studies, classical studies, folklore, history, journalism, language and literature, literary and political criticism, performing arts, philosophy, religion, and theology. (Note especially that history is covered by this index rather than by *Social Sciences Index*.) It is published quarterly with annual cumulations.

Business Periodicals Index (1958–).   This currently covers about 300 magazines and journals in the fields of accounting, advertising and marketing, automation, banking, communications, economics, finance and investment, insurance, labor, management, public relations, and taxation. It is especially valuable for picking up articles on individual companies and biographical articles about business leaders. It comes out quarterly with annual cumulations. Coverage prior to 1958 is provided by the *Industrial Arts Index* (1913–1957).

General Science Index (1978–).   A relatively new source, *GSI* covers about 90 English-language periodicals in the areas of astronomy, atmospheric sciences, biological sciences, botany, chemistry, earth sciences, environment and conservation, food and nutrition, genetics, mathematics, medicine and health, microbiology, oceanography, physics, physiology, psychology, and zoology. It appears monthly with various cumulations during the year, and with a hardbound permanent cumulation at the end. Unlike most other Wilson indexes, it provides only subject (not author) access.

Applied Science and Technology Index (1958–).   Another successor to *Industrial Arts Index* (1913–1957), this venerable source covers approximately 300 periodicals in the fields of aeronautics and space science, chemistry, computer technology and applications, construction industry, electricity, energy resources and research, engineering, environmental sciences, fire and fire prevention, food and food industry, geology, industrial and mechanical arts, machinery, mathematics, metallurgy, oceanography, petroleum and gas, physics, plastics, telecommunications, textile industry and fabrics, and transportation. Like *General Science Index*, it provides only subject (not author) access. It is a monthly publication with quarterly and annual cumulations.

Biological and Agricultural Index (1964–).   A successor to the *Agricultural Index* (1916–1963), this source indexes approximately 180 English-language periodicals in the areas of agricultural chemicals, agricultural economics, agricultural engineering, agronomy, animal husbandry, bacteriology, biology, botany, conservation, dairying, ecology, entomology, environmental sciences, food sciences, forestry, genetics, horticulture, livestock, marine biology, microbiology, mycology, nutrition, pesticides, physiology, poultry, soil science, veterinary medicine, virology, wildlife, and zoology. It appears quarterly with annual cumulations.

Index to Legal Periodicals (1908–   ). This set covers over 400 legal periodicals in the United States, Canada, Great Britain, Ireland, Australia, and New Zealand; it also picks up yearbooks, annual institutes, and annual reviews. The useful subheading "Cases" appears under specific subject headings, and there is also a separate "Table of Cases" section arranged by plaintiffs' names. It is published quarterly with annual and three-year cumulations; the latter two provide the list of subject headings and cross-references used in indexing.

Education Index (1929–   ). This covers approximately 330 English language publications in its field, including the areas of administration and supervision, adult education, the arts, audiovisual education, comparative and international education, counseling, personnel service, English language arts, health and physical education, higher education, language and linguistics, library and information science, multicultural/ethnic education, preschool and elementary education, psychology and mental health, religious education, science and mathematics, secondary education, social studies, special education and rehabilitation, teacher education, teaching methods and curriculum, and vocational education. Like *Social Sciences Index,* it has a very useful subject heading "Tests and scales." It is published monthly, with quarterly and annual cumulations.

Biography Index (1946–   ). This is more than just an index to journal literature. In addition to picking out the biographical materials from all of the more than 3000 periodicals that are covered by the other Wilson indexes, it also covers English language *books* of individual and collective biography, plus the *New York Times* obituaries. It is one of the best sources providing overall access to all types of biographical materials including autobiographies, bibliographies, critical studies, diaries, drama, fiction (biographical novels), interviews, journals, juvenile literature, letters, memoirs, pictorial works, and poetry. It also has an index by names of occupations and subject categories (e.g., "Architects," "Economists," "Handicapped," "Murder victims"). It comes out quarterly with annual and three-year cumulations.

Art Index (1929–   ).   The coverage of foreign language materials by this index is much better than the corresponding coverage of the other Wilson Indexes. *Art Index* picks up about 200 domestic and foreign art-related journals and museum bulletins, including coverage of archeology, architecture, art history, arts and crafts, city planning, fine arts, graphic arts, industrial design, interior design, landscape design, photography and film, and related subjects. It appears quarterly with annual cumulations.

The Wilson Company publishes a variety of other indexes, too (e.g., *Bibliographic Index, Book Review Digest, Library Literature, Play Index, Short Story Index, Children's Catalog, Fiction Catalog,* etc.), so this list is not complete. If you wish to find out if there is an index in some subject area not covered above, see Chapter 13.

The vocabulary control of the subject headings used in the Wilson indexes is worth noting. They have their own system of headings and cross-references within each index, so *it is especially important always to look for and follow "see also" references to other subject headings.* Beyond this, however, the indexes consult the *Library of Congress Subject Headings* list for much of their terminology. They are not limited to this list (hence the importance of following the cross-references); but they use it often enough that you should make use of the relationship. My own experience is that very frequently an *LCSH* heading that works in the card catalog *also* works in the Wilson indexes—and vice-versa. Four examples:

- A reader was interested in the matter of parents legally abdicating responsibility for rearing their children, but was having trouble finding a relevant subject heading. In looking through the *Index to Legal Periodicals,* however, she found several relevant titles of articles under the heading "Parent and child (Law)." She then tried this same heading in the card catalog and found pertinent books.

- A drama student interested in the avant-garde "Living Theatre" group of the 1960s found that the right subject heading to use in the *Humanities Index* is "Experimental theatre." She then used the same heading in both the card catalog and *Bibliographic Index* (a subject index to published bibliographies) and found more useful sources, among them Margaret Croyden's *Lunatics, Lovers and Poets: the Contemporary Experimental Theatre* (McGraw-Hill, 1974). This volume has a 45-page chapter on the Living Theatre, and an extensive bibliography.

- The woman who wanted material on the effects of divorce on children eventually found that the right subject heading to use in the card catalog is "Children of divorced parents" (and not "Divorce"). She then found that the same heading is used in the *Social Sciences Index* and in *Readers' Guide*.

- An example of the difference between *LCSH* and Wilson terminology is provided by the student who wanted material on job interviews. He found that the relevant *LCSH* term is "Employment interviewing," and this worked well in the card catalog. However, when he looked up the same term in *Business Periodicals Index* he found a note to *"see* Recruiting of employees—Interviewing"; and when he tried it in *Social Sciences Index* another note told him to *"see* Interviews and interviewing." Thus the Wilson indexes, here, did not use the *LCSH* term—however, the important point is that they still listed it and provided a cross-reference from it to their own terms. Starting with the *LCSH* list can still provide you with a hook into the vocabulary of the journal indexes. Again, this technique does not *always* work—but it works often enough that you should consciously make use of it.

A company that is in competition with Wilson is Information Access Corporation; it, too, publishes basic indexes—although not in as many subject fields as Wilson—but it adheres much more strictly and consistently to *Library of Congress Subject Headings*. These indexes are:

- *The Magazine Index.* This source, like the others from Information Access, is a self-contained microfilm reader with a roll of film that is changed every month. Each film is cumulative for the past three to five years, which saves you the trouble of repeating the same search in several annual volumes and monthly supplements. (The corresponding disadvantages are that you cannot simply photocopy the list of articles you find and that only one person at a time can use the index.) *Magazine Index* covers over 400 popular periodicals, including all of the approximately 180 that are in *Readers' Guide*.

- *The Business Index*.   This is more comprehensive than *Business Periodicals Index;* it covers more than 800 business periodicals cover-to-cover, including the *Wall Street Journal* and relevant articles from the *New York Times* and all business articles from more than 1000 general and legal periodicals, plus business *books*.

- *Legal Resource Index*.   This covers all articles in more than 700 legal periodicals, selected articles from 400 more general periodicals and newspapers, and legal monographs and government publications. In other words, it covers about twice what the corresponding Wilson index picks up.

Although these three provide broader coverage than their Wilson counterparts, fewer libraries will own them, whereas almost all will have the Wilsons.

The fact that so many of these basic indexes to journals use *Library of Congress Subject Headings* for their vocabulary control is especially important in cross-disciplinary inquiries. If you find a valid LC term, you can generally use it in an astonishing range of sources. The reason for this is that each index covers not merely the subject indicated in its title but, in addition, *other subjects from the perspective of that discipline*.[2] (Unfortunately, very few researchers ever exploit this fact.) To choose only one example, a researcher looking under "Indians of North America" would find much material in the card catalog and in *Social Sciences Index* and *Humanities Index*. But he would also find an amazing amount of coverage—under the same heading—in *Applied Science & Technology Index*, *Art Index*, *Biological and Agricultural Index*, *Business Periodicals Index*, *Education Index*, *Essay & General Literature Index*, *General Science Index*, *Index to Legal Periodicals*, *Readers' Guide*, *Business Index*, *Legal Resource Index*, and *Magazine Index*. (And, to press the inquiry on to other sources not discussed in detail so far, he could also use the same term in *Access* [a supplement to *Readers' Guide*], *American Book Publishing Record*, *Bibliographic Index*, *Cumulative Book Index*, *Fiction Catalog*, *Index to U.S. Government Periodicals*, *Monthly Catalog of U.S. Government Publications*, *National Newspaper Index*, *Public Affairs Information Service*, *Short Story Index*, and *Subject Collections* [a guide to libraries with special strengths in various subject areas].)

You could similarly use almost the full range of sources on many other subjects (e.g., Aged, Art, Blacks, Communications, Computers, Management, Religion, Shipwrecks, Tea, Underdeveloped areas, Women, et al.). The point is that virtually no subject is limited to a single index; rather, all the indexes may cover any subject, but from differing perspectives. And the relatively frequent use of *LCSH* terminology greatly facilitates parallel searches in different disciplines. My experience as a reference librarian is that the question "Which indexes use LC terms?" is often more important than "Which index covers *X* subject?"—for *dozens* of indexes may cover a particular topic, and if a researcher uses only one or two, then he may well miss more than he finds.

Sometimes the cross-disciplinary potential of the various indexes is surprising, as shown in the following examples:

- *Business Periodicals Index* picks up an article entitled "Case Study of a Decision Analysis: Hamlet's Soliloquy" from the journal *Interface*.

- *Legal Resource Index* cites a law review journal article on "Hamlet and the Law of Homicide," plus at least six other articles on Shakespeare.

- *General Science Index* locates an article on "Was Shakespeare a Playwright?" from *Science Digest*.

- *Index to U.S. Government Periodicals* has five articles under "Shakespeare" since 1979.

- *Biological and Agricultural Index,* too, within the last decade has three articles on the Shakespeare Gardens.

- A recent issue of *Applied Science & Technology Index* has cross-references under "Art" to "Architecture," "Ceramic art," and "Photography and sculpture"; under "Art and science" there is an article entitled "Robots Take the Lead in Ballet." Similarly, a recent volume of *General Science Index* has references under "Art" to the following:

  Animals in art
  Biological illustrations
  Birds in art
  Computers—Art uses
  Fish in art

　　Paintings
　　Plants in art

There are also articles or references under:

　　Art, Prehistoric
　　Art and mathematics
　　Art and mental illness
　　Art and science

Of course, in most cases a researcher will not need to use the full range of perspectives available on her subject (e.g., even though *Applied Science & Technology Index* does cover "Indians of North America," the reader may be quite satisfied with what she finds in only *Social Sciences Index* and *Humanities Index*). Nevertheless, I think it is important for researchers to realize how many indexes outside their own discipline may cover articles within their area of interest— for, given that you must "draw the line" somewhere in bringing an inquiry to a close, it is preferable to be able to *choose a stopping point while knowing what the options are for continuing* rather than to *have to stop because you have run out of ideas*.

A knowledge of which indexes use LC subject headings will thus greatly extend the range of options that most people will consider, and for this reason a familiarity with the Wilson and Information Access indexes is especially useful for basic library research.

Unfortunately, you must also remember that "a little knowledge is a dangerous thing." The basic indexes just mentioned are not the end of the line. Indeed, the specialized indexes may not be the end, either. The problem is that many researchers—and I include graduate students and professors especially—believe that the few or "basic" sources within their discipline that they are aware of are the *only* ones available, or that the same few are the *best* ones for all searches. Neither assumption is trustworthy. There will always be scores of access tools you've never heard of unless you are a full-time reference generalist— and even being a full professor by no means guarantees familiarity with the range of information resources in that field, let alone the amazing variety of sources in all other tangential fields. (Indeed, a number of studies have demonstrated that academics use indexes only sparingly, and that they usually arrive at the limits of their research when they have merely followed up footnotes in known sources and browsed a few areas of the bookstacks.)

Librarians frequently notice the problem with *Readers' Guide to Periodical Literature*. Probably half of the people who use it do so only because they are unaware of the existence of the more specialized indexes (and, too, they've been told that they "should know how to find things on their own" so they don't ask for guidance). The same problem also occurs with each of the other indexes I've listed—and with others I could have mentioned. For example:

- A researcher in the social sciences will certainly want to know about the *Social Sciences Index*, and will probably want to start there rather than in *Readers' Guide*. However, many other indexes in this broad field would be much better for many searches. The *Public Affairs Information Service Bulletin (P.A.I.S.)*, for instance, is much more comprehensive on matters of public policy and political and international affairs (and it, too, tends to use *LCSH* terminology). Similarly, the most comprehensive index in psychology is not *Social Sciences Index* but *Psychological Abstracts*. Some researchers will be better served by *Sociological Abstracts, Anthropology Literature*, the *New York Times Index*, or the annual *Handbook of Latin American Studies*. And there are many more that may be of even greater use, depending on the search topic.

- *Humanities Index* is not always the best source for searches in its broad field. The *MLA International Bibliography* is the most comprehensive general index to critical articles on literary works; but for even better coverage of, say, the Romantic movement you should use the annual *Romantic Movement: A Selective and Critical Bibliography*. And *Historical Abstracts* is the best ongoing index to sources on world history other than American; and *America: History and Life* is the best for American history; but the *Combined Retrospective Index to Journals in History 1838–1974* may be better than either in some cases. And then there are other specialized humanistic sources such as *Philosopher's Index, Catholic Periodical and Literature Index*, and many more.

- *Applied Science and Technology Index* is not as comprehensive in its broad area as *Engineering Index* nor as specialized in the aerospace field as *International Aerospace Abstracts*. Nor is the *Biological and Agricultural Index* as comprehensive as *Biological Abstracts, Index Medicus*, or the National Agricultural Library's *Bibliography of Agriculture*, each of which is the best overall index in its field (although not necessarily the best *specialized* index for a *particular* field within its broad coverage—e.g., *Sport Fishery Abstracts* includes more in its narrow area than does *Biological Abstracts*).

- *Business Periodicals Index* is not the end of the line in its area, either—the *Predicasts F & S Index*es (*United States, Europe,* and *International*), the *Wall Street Journal Index, Business Index, Accountant's Index, Journal of Economic Literature,* and *Personnel Literature* (among many others) may well be better for many searches.

These lists could be extended considerably. There are easy ways to find out which specialized indexes exist (see Chapter 13); but the ability to do research involves more than your having a knowledge of a few finding aids, no matter how comprehensive they are. What are most important are your initial *assumptions* about what is *likely* to exist. If you start out by assuming that only general information on a subject exists or that only general indexes are available, then you are likely to formulate your questions only in general terms and to stop your research when you have used only the most superfical access tools. If you don't know in advance that you should look for specific (not general) subject headings, and if you don't know in advance something of the range of specific (not general) indexes available, then you will probably miss much more than you find and then give up searching too soon in the mistaken belief that *Readers' Guide* has covered everything.

A knowledge of at least the Wilson indexes in all the specialized subject areas, however, should get you past the roadblock of thinking only in general terms. If you know enough about a few specialized sources to seek them out in the first place, then right there you will be greatly increasing the efficiency of your research. Your basic assumption should be that if you want specific information *it is more efficient to start by looking for the specific* and *then* to broaden your search as necessary, *rather than to start with the broad and narrow down to the specific.* The information storage-retrieval-indexing system allows you to proceed in *either* direction, of course; but comparatively few researchers seem to realize this—most think of a search strategy only in the direction of general to specific. And yet most would get much better retrieval results by proceeding in the opposite direction.

A question that often comes up regarding periodicals is that of finding where a particular journal is indexed—that is, which indexes will provide subject (or other) access to the one journal in which you are interested. A number of sources are particularly useful in supplying this information:

1. *Ulrich's International Periodicals Directory* (formerly irregular, now annual). This is a list of over 60,000 periodicals published all over the world; the entries are listed in alphabetical subject groups, which facilitates finding which journals are currently being published in particular fields. Each entry provides bibliographic information on the journal, and gives the address of the publisher and the price of a subscription; it also tells you which indexes cover that journal.

2. *Irregular Serials and Annuals.* Irregularly published itself, this list is a good supplement to *Ulrich's.* It covers "proceedings, transactions, advances, progresses, reports, yearbooks, handbooks, annual reviews, and monographic series, which constitute the 'twilight' area between books and serials." It is arranged like *Ulrich's* and provides similar information for its entries.

3. *Chicorel Index to Abstracting and Indexing Services* (Chicorel Index Series, vols. 11 and 11A; 2nd ed., 1978). These two volumes list journals in the humanities and social sciences and tell where they are indexed.

4. *Indexed Periodicals: A Guide to 170 Years of Coverage in 33 Indexing Services,* by Joseph Marconi (Pierian Press, 1976). This is most useful for finding index coverage for older periodicals; for current information, a combination of the other sources is preferable.

5. *Magazines for Libraries,* by Bill Katz and Linda Sternberg Katz (Bowker, revised irregularly). Less comprehensive than *Ulrich's,* this volume still has an advantage in that it provides paragraph annotations for all the journals listed; it also tells you which are the *best* journals in any subject field, whereas *Ulrich's* simply lists them all.

6. *Serials for Libraries: An Annotated Guide to Continuations, Annuals, Yearbooks, Almanacs, Transactions, Proceedings, Directories, Services,* edited by John V. Ganly and Diane M. Sciattara

(2nd ed.; New York: Neal-Schuman Publishers, 1985). This is to *Irregular Serials* what Katz is to *Ulrich's;* it provides critical annotations to assist librarians (and others) in collection development.

7. *Standard Periodical Directory* (Oxbridge Communications, irregular). This is the largest listing of magazines and journals published in the United States.

8. *Serials Directory* (EBSCO, annual). This is a new international directory that includes 113,000 regular serials, annuals, and irregulars in one listing.

9. Catalog records for serials contained in the OCLC database (see Chapter 9) often contain a "510 note field" that will tell you which of 136 different indexes cover the title you want. This note field is frequently quite lengthy.

10. "Author's Guide" volumes that discuss the style requirements of journals in particular subject areas also frequently mention which indexes cover the journals (see Appendix).

All these sources are useful in listing where a journal or serial is indexed, although some of them provide such information only spottily. It is important to remember that you have to use a *combination* of them—studies done by librarians have shown that none of the hard copy sources is complete (or, in some cases, even correct) by itself.

Many hundreds of journals are simply not indexed anywhere; nevertheless, you may wish to be aware of their existence since the information contained in them may still be of great value of you. To find out all the journals being published in any subject area, use *Ulrich's* and *Irregular Serials,* supplemented by the *Standard Periodical Directory,* the *Serials Directory,* and the *Gale Directory of Publications* (Gale, annual). The combination of these five will give you a virtually complete roster of current journals, house publications, and newspapers, with subscription information for each (and subject access by broad categories). The *Standard* is preferable to *Ulrich's* for listing periodicals currently published in the United States; *Gale* provides the best coverage of U.S. newspapers.

To find out which periodicals are considered the best or the most important in their areas, use the combination of Katz and Ganly, and the *Journal Citation Reports* volumes of the ISI indexes (see Chapter 6).

It is important for researchers to realize that libraries catalog serials and journals differently from monographs. It is not efficient to create separate catalog cards for each issue of every journal; a more sensible practice is to catalog the journal as a whole once, with one catalog number for the whole run, and then simply to check in each new issue or bound volume as it comes in. Because of the constant checking and claiming of missing issues that must go on, the serials record catalog is always separate from the main card file of a library and is usually located right near the cataloging department. The main card catalog itself will record the titles of journals—but you need more information than this. You also want to check the library's *holdings* of the journal you're interested in—that is, does the library own the particular *volume* or *year* that you want? Libraries will not own complete sets of all titles represented in their catalogs, so it is important to find out in advance which volumes you can expect to find. The card for a journal in the main catalog will *not* indicate the library's *holdings*. The date of publication given on this card will usually be that of volume 1, whether or not the library actually owns volume 1 or a complete set after it. (This date is simply for identification purposes, to distinguish between journals with the same title.) When you want to find whether a library has the journal indicated in a citation you've found, check the *serials record rather than the main card catalog,* or you may waste a lot of time searching for "missing" or "not on shelf" volumes that the library never owned in the first place. (Reference librarians quite frequently encounter frustrated readers engaged in just such searches.)

Another frustrating problem that researchers often have with serials is one that can usually be prevented with a bit of foresight. The entries in most of the journal indexes give you a bibliographic citation to the journal articles, but they usually abbreviate the titles of the journals. Each index *also* has a separate section that expands these abbreviations into the full wording of the complete title, and it is very important to write down these *full titles rather than abbreviations.* If all you have is an abbreviation, you will have trouble looking up the title in the library's catalogs (e.g., "Educ" can stand for "Education" or "Educationa*l*," which file differently; "Ann" can be "Ann*ual*" or "An-na*ls*"; "Com" can be "Com*munity*" or "Com*merce*"; "Soc" can be "Soc*iety*" or "Soc*ial*"; "Res" can be "Res*ources*" or "Re-se*arch*"; etc.[3]). The small words that are left out can also cause problems. One researcher looking for *Bull. Hist. Med.* assumed that it means *Bulletin of Historical Medicine.* It doesn't—it's *Bulletin of the*

History of Medicine. Note from the boldface letters how far apart the two would be in word-by-word filing—in looking for the first form, the researcher was nowhere near the locale of the journal he really wanted. A wise researcher, in copying a citation, will therefore *never abbreviate the title of a journal. Never.* The few extra seconds it takes to look up the full title (from the list at the front of the index volume) may save you literally hours of verifying at a later date—especially if you are looking for the article in a library other than the one in which you wrote down the citation.

Another problem with serials has been mentioned before in Chapter 2, but bears repeating here: there has been a change in the cataloging rules as of January 1, 1981. Under the new rules, a journal such as *Journal of the American Medical Association* is entered under just this title. Under the old rules, however, it would appear as *American Medical Association. Journal.* The old rule was that *if the name of the organization appears in the title,* then file under the first word of the *name* and not under the first word (e.g., *Journal, Annals, Bulletin, Proceedings,* etc.) of the title. This obviously caused—and continues to cause—much confusion, as it leads many researchers who look under the wrong form to conclude that a library does not own a particular serial when it actually is available. Most libraries are going through a trying period right now, having to decide whether to recatalog their old files under the new rules (a very expensive operation) or to set up two files with cross-references between them. The important point is that you should be aware of the necessity of looking under both forms of entry.

Notes

1. Subsequent information on the individual indexes is derived mainly from a free pamphlet available from the Wilson Company, entitled *Indexing and Cataloging Services of the H. W. Wilson Company.*

2. The same point can be made about specialized encyclopedias.

3. A study by John Martin and Alan Gilchrist, *An Evaluation of British Scientific Journals* (ASLIB, 1968), found that in the *Science Citation Index* citing authors abbreviated *Proceedings of the Institute of Electrical Engineers* 24 different ways.

5

Key Word Searches

The Wilson and Information Access indexes discussed in the previous chapter are of the subject heading or controlled vocabulary type. The advantage of such an indexing method is that it solves the problem of synonyms (e.g., "Death penalty," "Capital punishment") and variant forms of expression (e.g., "Fraudulent advertising," "Advertising, fraudulent")—because of the principle of uniform heading it groups together under one term works that treat the same subject but refer to it by different words. This grouping function saves you the considerable trouble of having to look in a wide variety of places for material on one subject.

But there are corresponding disadvantages to a controlled vocabulary system. First, the grouping function is sometimes achieved at the expense of blurring fine distinctions between subjects. One reader, for example, was interested in the idea of "patients actively participating in the therapeutic process." The LC subject heading that includes material on this topic is "Patient compliance"—which is not quite the same thing as "active patient participation." Still, it is close enough that the catalogers apparently decided to use it rather than to create a new heading. Another example is provided by the researcher who wanted material on "Subfractional horsepower electric motors." I showed her the *LCSH* heading "Electric motors, Fractional horsepower," but she insisted that she wanted only *sub*fractional and *not* fractional. When we looked at the cards under the "Fractional" heading, however, we

saw that it included works on subfractional motors. Evidently, the catalogers, seeing no separate heading in the list for "Subfractional,"
simply chose the closest heading that did exist. This often happens.
*Distinctions that are important to subject specialists may not be per-
ceived as important by library catalogers; and if you want to retrieve
library materials you must think in the terms used by the catalogers,
not the subject specialists.* LCSH headings thus often include subjects
that are not precisely indicated by the terminology of the heading.

Second, a controlled vocabulary system frequently cannot get too
specific within one subject. This is particularly true of the card catalog, which seeks to summarize the content of works as a whole (i.e.,
the principle of co-extensivity, rather than indexing individual parts,
sections, or chapters of a book). Thus the researcher who was looking
for material on the dental identification of Hitler's deputy Martin Bormann could find a general heading on "Bormann, Martin, 1900–   ,"
but not a precise one on "Dental identification of Martin Bormann."
Similarly, a researcher looking for "Effects of wing design on reduc-
ing heat stress at supersonic speeds in military aircraft" will not find
a controlled vocabulary term that is nearly as precise as he would
wish. The whole idea of such a controlled system is to create *groups*
of records; and groups by their very nature have to have more than
one item in them.

Third, controlled vocabularies are also by nature rather conservative
and slow to change. The main reason for this is that a cataloger cannot
simply insert a new term into the list without integrating it with the
existing terms through a web of cross-references that must extend *from*
the new word to the others, and *to* the new word from the others, with
broader/narrower relationships defined in both directions. This takes
considerable effort, and so catalogers are cautious about acting too
quickly—they find it is often advisable to wait until the new subject
comes to standardize its own vocabulary first. And so if your subject
is in a new field, or is of recent development, its terms may not yet
appear in the system. An example is provided by Leon Festinger's
groundbreaking book *A Theory of Cognitive Dissonance* (Row and Peterson, 1957) which opened up a whole new field of psychology. It
was not until several years later that the precise term "Cognitive dissonance" became a fixed subject heading in the vocabulary of *Psychological Abstracts*—thus for a time the literature of a developing field
was not easily accessible.

Fourth, the cross-reference structure of a controlled vocabulary system may not be adequate to get you from the terms you know to the heading that is acceptable. For example, *Psychological Abstracts* has always indexed articles on the psychological problems of hostages released by terrorists; but a few years ago (prior to the phenomenon's becoming relatively common) its thesaurus of subject headings did not include cross-references from the terms "Hostages" or "Terrorism" to the subject heading that it uses instead (see Chapter 9).

The problems for researchers, then, are these: What do you do when there is no subject heading that corresponds to what you want to find? Or what do you do when the cross-references are inadequate to lead you to the heading that does exist somewhere in the list?

So far we have seen two methods of circumventing such limitations of controlled vocabularies: you can look for likely *titles* rather than subject headings, as they may be more precise; and you can systematically browse materials arranged in a subject classification scheme. Both methods work for books, but they involve a lot of hit-or-miss searching. And neither works for journal articles, as citations to these are not accessible by title within conventional indexes, nor are the articles themselves arranged in logical groupings on the shelves.

But there are a number of *un*conventional indexes that can solve the problem of there being no subject heading for what you want. The three most important of these are:

1. *Science Citation Index* (1955–   ); quarterly with annual and five-year cumulations.   This huge index covers over 3000 journals in all fields of science, plus another 3000 nonscience journals insofar as they have science-related articles. (It should be noted, though, that for the ten years 1955–1964 many fewer journals are indexed—coverage in the thousands extends only from the mid-1960s to the present. A further note: while citation searching is possible from 1955 to date, the key word index first appears in 1966.)

2. *Social Sciences Citation Index* (1966–   ); quarterly with annual annual and five-year cumulations.   This provides complete coverage of about 1500 journals in all fields of the social sciences, plus selective coverage of about 4500 others in sciences and humanities.

3. *Arts & Humanities Citation Index* (1975–   ); published three times a year with annual and five-year cumulations.   This provides cover-to-cover indexing of over 1300 journals in its broad fields, plus

selective coverage of the science and social science journals insofar as they have humanities articles (e.g., papers on electronic music in the technical journals).

All three are published by the Institute for Scientific Information (ISI) in Philadelphia.

The value of these indexes is that *they provide two methods of circumventing the limitations of subject heading indexes,* through *key word searching* and *citation searching,* both of which involve much less hit-or-miss scanning than the other alternatives.

Each issue of an ISI index, whether quarterly, annual, or five-year cumulation, is itself a multivolume set consisting essentially of a "Permuterm" Subject index, a Source index, and a Citation index. The first of these is an alphabetical list of all significant or key words from the titles of all journal articles covered by that issue, and arranged in such a way that if you look up one word you can tell if any other word of interest appeared with it in the title of an article. This allows for great precision in searching.

For example, one reader looking for articles on "Managing sociotechnical change" had a problem with the conventional indexes because no subject heading reaches this concept efficiently—the "Management" term in *LCSH* covers too wide a field. However, with the *Social Sciences Citation Index* (or *SSCI*), the reader could look up the precise word "sociotechnical" to see if it appears with the words "managing" or "management" in the title of someone's journal article. It does—there are at least ten hits that are right on the button. Similarly, a researcher interested in "the administrative position of the Captaincy in colonial Brazil" couldn't find a precise enough *LCSH* heading; however, with the ISI indexes he could look up "Captaincy" to see if it appears with "Brazil" in a journal article title. And it does. And the reader who couldn't find articles on "Hostages" in *Psychological Abstracts* simply had to look up that precise word in the *SSCI* to find over a score of hits.

Key word searches thus frequently allow much more precise retrieval than subject heading searches; and as an alternative to the latter they involve much less hit-or-miss searching than does the technique of browsing or using a classification scheme. With a key word search you can zero in very quickly to the exact words you are looking for.

There is a trade-off involved, however. The price you pay for such precise access is the loss of synonym control—that is, with key word indexes you *do* have to think up all of the variant ways in which a subject can be expressed. If, for example, you look up only the words "capital" and "punishment," you will miss all the citations that use the terms "death penalty" or "execution" or "death row." And there will be *no cross-references* to lead you from one term to the other. Similarly you must be careful to look up variant singular, plural, and possessive forms of the same word (e.g., "child," "child's," "children," "children's"). Such problems are solved for you in subject heading indexes—that is the peculiar strength of controlled vocabularies. Their weakness is that they often lack precise enough terms, or terms that are up-to-date; but here the key word sources have their peculiar strength. The advantages and disadvantages of the two types of indexes are thus neatly complementary.

All researchers should at least be aware of the three basic ISI indexes, for collectively they provide access to all subject areas through a key word approach. These three, however, are by no means the only sources offering key word access to knowledge records. Some of the others are:

ISSHP: Index to Social Sciences & Humanities Proceedings
ISTP: Index to Scientific and Technical Proceedings
ISR: Index to Scientific Reviews
ISBC: Index to Scientific Book Contents
CMCI Compu/Math Citation Index
Comprehensive Dissertation Index
Combined Retrospective Index to Journals in History 1838–1974
Combined Retrospective Index to Journals in Political Science 1886–1974
Combined Retrospective Index to Journals in Sociology 1895–1974
Biological Abstracts
Transdex
Monthly Catalog of U.S. Government Publications (key word index from 1980–   )
Publications Reference File
Government Reports Announcements & Index
NTIS Title Index on Microfiche

The first five of these are also published by the Institute for Scientific Information. The last five cover government publications and will be discussed in more detail in Chapter 12.

What is more important than remembering a list of specific titles, however, is that you remember the *technique* of key word searching with its advantages and disadvantages, as an alternative to subject heading searches. And—just as with subject heading indexes—each of these key word sources covers many subjects beyond whatever area of concentration may be mentioned in its title (e.g., "Women" and "Computers" can be found in *all* of them). No matter what your subject, in other words, *several* key word indexes will cover it. You can always assume that this method of searching is available for pursuing an inquiry.

As I mentioned earlier, a reference librarian often finds that the first question to ask is whether or not a good subject heading exists that corresponds to a researcher's need; if there is one, then a whole class of sources can be brought to bear on the problem. But if there isn't, then we can readily shift gears and use another approach that involves a distinctly different class of sources: key word indexes.

Nor is this approach confined to journal indexes. The key word search capability is involved in many alternatives:

- Dictionaries.
- Encyclopedias (especially those with a separate index volume).
- Card catalog (i.e., by looking for the first word of a book's title as a key word).
- Index pages at the ends of monographs.
- Browsing through texts of books.
- Manual key word indexes such as those described above.
- Computer searches (see Chapter 9).
- *The Encyclopedia of Associations* (key word index).
- Talking to people (see Chapter 11).

All these methods and sources allow you to get around the problem of not finding a good subject heading for what you want.

The three basic ISI indexes should be kept in mind especially by scholars who wish to pursue cross-disciplinary inquiries. Each of them covers a vast range of subjects, and so brings to bear on any inquiry a huge range of journals from many disciplines. The *Science Citation Index,* for example, covers journals in all the following fields:

Acoustics

Aerospace Engineering and
    Technology

Agricultural Economics and
    Policy

Agricultural Experiment Station
    Reports

Agriculture

Agriculture, Dairy, and Animal
    Science

Agriculture, Soil Science

Allergy

Anatomy and Morphology

Andrology

Anesthesiology

Astronautics

Astronomy and Astrophysics

Behavioral Sciences

Biochemistry and Molecular
    Biology

Biology

Biophyics

Botany

Cancer

Cardiovascular System

Chemistry

Chemistry, Analytical

Chemistry, Applied

Chemistry, Inorganic and
    Nuclear

Chemistry, Organic

Chemistry, Physical

Computer Applications and
    Cybernetics

Construction and Building
    Technology

Crystallography

Cytology and Histology

Dentistry and Odontology

Dermatology and Venereal
    Diseases

Drugs and Addiction

Ecology

Education, Scientific
    Disciplines

Electrochemistry

Embryology

Endocrinology and Metabolism

Energy and Fuels

Engineering

Engineering, Biomedical

Engineering, Chemical

Engineering, Civil

Engineering, Electrical and
    Electronic

Engineering, Mechanical

Entomology

Environmental Sciences

Ergonomics

Fisheries

Food Science and Technology

Forestry

Gastroenterology

Genetics and Heredity

Geography

Geology

Geosciences

Geriatrics and Gerontology

Hematology
History and Philosophy of
    Science
Horticulture
Hygiene and Public Health
Immunology
Information Science and
    Library Science
Instruments and Instrumentation
Limnology
Marine and Freshwater Biology
Materials Science
Materials Science, Ceramics
Materials Science, Paper and
    Wood
Mathematics
Mathematics, Applied
Mathematics, Miscellaneous
Mechanics
Medical Laboratory Technology
Medicine, General and Internal
Medicine, Miscellaneous
Medicine, Research and
    Experimental
Metallurgy and Mining
Meteorology and Atmospheric
    Sciences
Microbiology
Microscopy
Mineralogy
Multidisciplinary Sciences
Mycology
Neurosciences
Nuclear Science and
    Technology
Nutrition and Dietetics
Obstetrics and Gynecology
Operations Research and
    Management Science

Opthalmology
Optics
Ornithology
Orthopedics
Otorhinolaryngology
Paleontology
Parasitology
Pathology
Pediatrics
Pharmacology and Pharmacy
Photographic Technology
Physics
Physics, Applied
Physics, Atomic, Molecular,
    and Chemical
Physics, Condensed Matter
Physics, Fluids and Plasmas
Physics, Mathematical
Physics, Miscellaneous
Physics, Nuclear
Physics, Particles and Fields
Physiology
Polymer Science
Psychiatry
Psychology
Radiology and Nuclear
    Medicine
Respiratory System
Rheumatology
Spectroscopy
Statistics and Probability
Surgery
Telecommunications
Toxicology
Urology and Nephrology
Veterinary Medicine
Virology
Water Resources
Zoology

A rather impressive list![1] The fact to note is that journals in *all* these disciplines are brought to bear simultaneously on any problem being researched with the *Science Citation Index*.

Similarly, the *Social Sciences Citation Index* covers all the following fields:

Anthropology
Archaeology
Area Studies
Business
Business, Finance
Communication
Criminology and Penology
Demography
Drugs and Addiction
Economics
Education and Educational
    Research
Education, Special
Environmental Studies
Ergonomics
Ethnic Studies
Family Studies
Geography
Geriatrics and Gerontology
Health Policy and Services
History
History and Philosophy of
    Science
History of Social Sciences
Hygiene and Public Health
Industrial Relations and
    Labor
Information Science and
    Library Science
International Relations

Language and Linguistics
Law
Management
Nursing
Philosophy
Planning and Development
Political Science
Psychiatry
Psychology
Psychology, Applied
Psychology, Clinical
Psychology, Developmental
Psychology, Educational
Psychology, Experimental
Psychology, Mathematical
Psychology, Social
Public Administration
Rehabilitation
Religion
Social Issues
Social Sciences, Biomedical
Social Sciences,
    Interdisciplinary
Social Sciences, Mathematical
    Methods
Social Work
Sociology
Transportation
Urban Studies
Women's Studies

And the *Arts & Humanities Citation Index* brings to bear on any topic journals in all the following fields:

Archaeology	Language and Linguistics
Architecture	Literary Reviews
Art	Literature
Arts and Humanities, General	Music
Classics	Oriental Studies
Dance	Philosophy
Film, Radio, Television	Poetry
Folklore	Religion
History	Theater

Collectively, the three ISI indexes summon the cross-disciplinary resources of approximately 6000 journals in all fields for use on any subject that may interest you.

This chapter has been concerned with the key word search capability of the ISI indexes; the next will consider their citation search capabilities.

Note

1. This list and the two that follow are taken from the prefatory material of the ISI indexes themselves.

6

Citation Searches

We have seen that the techniques of controlled vocabulary searching, systematic browsing, and key word searching each have advantages and disadvantages. There is still another method of doing a subject search that is potentially applicable in any field: citation searching. And it, too, has peculiar strengths and limitations.

In citation searching you must start with a known source. It may be a book, a journal article, a conference paper, a dissertation, a technical report—it can be any kind of knowledge record, and it can have been published last year or centuries ago. It doesn't matter. What a citation search will tell you is whether someone has written a subsequent journal article which cites that source in a footnote, as a follow-up discussion of it or at least reference to it. The assumption is that a later work which cites an earlier one is probably talking about the same subject, and this usually proves to be the case.

The same three ISI indexes that were discussed in connection with key word searches are also the basic sources for citation searching:

1. *Science Citation Index* (1955–   )
2. *Social Sciences Citation Index* (1966–   )
3. *Arts & Humanities Citation Index* (1975–   )

Suppose, for instance, that you are using the 1980 set of the *SSCI*. If you already have a book or article on your subject (whether published in 1979, 1920, or 1725), the 1980 *SSCI* will tell you if someone has written a journal article in 1980—in any of the almost 1500 periodicals covered by the index—which cites that source in a footnote. (Note that monographs can be cit*ed* sources but not cit*ing*).

An example is provided by the reader who was interested in the Norse colonization of America before Columbus. He had already found one good scholarly article discussing the evidence; but on running it through the *SSCI* he found a subsequent article by another scholar who disagreed with the conclusions of the first. And this was followed by a rebuttal by the original writer. The combination of perspectives developed by this dialog brought about considerable information that did not appear in the first article by itself.

A more striking example of follow-up discussion is provided by the book mentioned earlier, Festinger's *Theory of Cognitive Dissonance* (1957). Just about every psychologist writing in this area starts out by referring to this original study. According to the *SSCI*, it was cited 139 times in 1976; in 1977, 125 times; in 1978, 130 times; in 1979, 112 times; in 1980, 127 times; and so on. A researcher could thus very easily see who is writing in this field in any given year.

The real advantage of citation searches should be apparent in relation to what has been said of the other methods: with citation searching you do not have to find the right subject heading or worry about the adequacy of cross-references, nor do you have to think up all relevant key words and variant phrasings—*because there is no vocabulary involved at all*. Moreover, these searches are usually more directly efficient than the hit-or-miss results that browsing produces. There are, of course, limitations as well: you must already have a good source to start with; and there is no guarantee that the best sources are linked by citations—it is quite possible that good works were produced entirely independently of each other. Again, then, no one method will find everything. Each is very likely to find something the others missed, but a combination of methods is needed for thoroughness.

A particularly useful "wrinkle" on citation searches is to cycle sources—that is, once you have found a first tier of articles that cites your original source, you can then find who cited *them*. This will give you a second tier; you can then see who cited them, which will provide a third tier, and so on. By pursuing this process as far as it will go you can sometimes develop an incredible amount of information on even the most obscure subjects.

While the ISI indexes are very useful in enabling you to follow the development of a debate or the growth of a scholarly discussion, they are also very helpful when the various book review indexes fail—for there is still a chance that the book you're interested in may have been commented on, or referred to critically or favorably, in a journal article even if it hasn't been formally reviewed. The ISI indexes also provide the best way of finding a "review" of a journal article, as these are not covered by book review indexes. And they are especially useful for giving a new lease on life to the materials you locate through old bibliographies—if the latter refer you to somewhat dated articles, you can find out if someone has used them as background sources for a new look at the subject. It is particularly worthwhile to see if anyone has cited old state-of-the-art review articles (see Chapter 7).

These indexes sometimes play a part, too, in academic circles on questions of promotion or tenure, for departments wish to know not only whether a candidate has published, but also if he or she has been cited by other scholars in the field. (And this has led, predictably, to some scholars getting their friends to cite their works to artificially inflate the count.)

Several other citation indexes are published by Shepard's/McGraw-Hill in the legal field; for these, the cited materials include:

Cases in United States Supreme Court Reports
Cases in federal reports (including administrative agency decisions and orders)
Cases in state reports
Cases in the National Reporter System
Opinions of the Attorneys General
United States Constitution
United States Code
United States Statutes at Large
United States Treaties and other international agreements
Code of Federal Regulations
Federal Court Rules
State Constitutions
State Codes
State Session Laws
Municipal Charters
Ordinances

State Court Rules
Jury Instructions
Restatement
Legal Periodicals
Standards of Criminal Justice
Patents
Trademarks
Copyrights

The cit*ing* materials include:

Cases in United States Supreme Court Reports
Cases in federal reports (including administrative agency decisions
    and orders)
Cases in state reports
Cases in the National Reporter System
Opinions of the Attorneys General
Articles in legal periodicals
Annotations in the American Law Reports[1]

Again, it is important that you remember the advantages and limitations of the *technique*, and perhaps the three basic ISI indexes. The others can be found with the help of reference librarians.

Four other points about the ISI indexes are worth noting:

1. They provide access to articles through the author's organizational affiliation—that is, you can find out who at any institution (such as a university) has published a paper in any given year, through the use of the *Corporate Source Index* volumes within each ISI set.

2. The *Science Citation Index* and the *Social Sciences Citation Index* both include a separate volume called *Journal Citation Reports*. These volumes present elaborate statistical data on which journals are being most frequently cited by other journals, both in general and within specialized fields. In other words, they provide rankings of how important a journal is based on the amount of discussion it generates in other journals.

3. ISI offers a service whereby for a fee you can order a copy of any post-1981 journal article covered by one of their indexes, in case

you cannot find one in a library. It's called "The Genuine Article" service; its 24-hour hotline number is 1-215-386-4399.

4. Cross-disciplinary inquiries can be pursued through the citation search method in a way that will give results unlike those achieved through subject heading or key word search methods—that is, sometimes you will find that a given source on a particular subject is unexpectedly cited by journals in completely different fields.[2] Such connections can be discovered only by citation indexes.

Notes

1. The above lists are quoted from the booklet *How to Use Shepard's Citations* (Shepard's/McGraw-Hill, 1980); free copies of this are available from the publisher at P.O. Box 1235, Colorado Springs, Colo. 80901.

2. Eugene Garfield, in his book *Citation Indexing: Its Theory and Application in Science, Technology, and Humanities* (John Wiley & Sons, 1979), mentions a spectacular example: "From 1961 to 1969 a citation for one of the classic papers published by Albert Einstein in *Annallen der Physik* in 1906 is linked [by the *Science Citation Index*] to papers from the *Journal of Dairy Sciences, Journal of the Chemical Society, Journal of Polymer Science, Journal of Pharmacy and Pharmacology, Comparative Biochemistry and Physiology, Journal of General Physiology, International Journal of Engineering Science, Journal of Materials, Journal of the Water Pollution Control Federation, American Ceramic Society Bulletin, Journal of the Acoustical Society of America, Chemical Engineering Science, Industrial and Engineering Chemistry Process Design and Development, Journal of Colloid and Interface Science, Journal of Fluid Mechanics, Journal of Lubrication Technology, Journal of Molecular Biology, Journal of Food Science, Journal of Biological Chemistry, Journal of Sedimentary Petrology, Review of Scientific Instruments,* and the *Journal of the Electrochemical Society.*"

7

Higher Level Overviews: Review Articles

Researchers are especially well advised to look for a particular type or subset of journal articles called review articles. These are not at all the same as book reviews and should not be confused with them. Review articles are a type of literature unto themselves in which the author tries to systematically read all the relevant literature on a subject (and sometimes also to interview the experts in the field) and then to organize, synthesize, and critically evaluate the range of information. His or her goal is to provide a state-of-the-art situation assessment of knowledge in the particular field and sometimes to indicate areas that need further research. A review article is somewhat like an encyclopedia article in trying to present an overview of a subject, but there are two important differences: (1) it is often written for specialists rather than laypeople, and so may assume familiarity with technical jargon; and (2) its bibliography will usually be exhaustive rather than selective or merely introductory.

In other words, if you are doing serious research and can find a review article on your subject, you're in great shape. There are several sources to check.

Index to Scientific Reviews or *ISR* (1974– ; semiannual). This is "An Interdisciplinary Index to the Review Literature of Science, Medicine, Agriculture, Technology, and the Behavioral Sciences." It is published by the Institute for Scientific Information, and it provides four avenues of access: by Permuterm Subject (i.e., key words from titles), Research Front Specialty, Author, and Corporate Source. You can use key words or personal authors as entry points, then find a set of additional relevant review articles with the Research Front Specialty Index. The latter groups together citations to those articles that are related to each other by the fact that they share a common cluster of footnotes; it is a way of searching, in other words, that circumvents the need to think up all relevant key words. Coverage includes over 3000 journals, plus over 200 of the hardbound annual volumes that are variously titled *Annual Review of . . . , Advances in . . . , Progress in . . . , Report of . . . , Research in . . .* , etc.

Annual Review of . . . (series). Annual Reviews, Inc., based in California, publishes many different series of review articles in various fields. All of them are indexed by the *Index to Scientific Reviews;* however, if your library doesn't subscribe to the *ISR* it may still have the sources you want and you can look directly at their own indexes. The titles are: *Annual Review of Anthropology; of Astronomy and Astrophysics; of Biochemistry; of Biophysics and Bioengineering; of Earth and Planetary Science; of Ecology and Systematics; of Energy; of Entomology; of Fluid Mechanics; of Genetics; of Intelligence and Affectivity; of Materials Science; of Medicine; of Microbiology; of Neuroscience; of Nuclear and Particle Science; of Pharmacology and Toxicology; of Physical Chemistry; of Physiology; of Phytopathology; of Plant Physiology; of Psychology; of Public Health; of Sociology.* The other series mentioned above (*Advances in . . . , Progress in . . .* , etc.) cover still other subjects. The best way to find out if a review series exists for your area of interest is to consult *Irregular Serials and Annuals,* which lists all of them by subject and also alphabetically by title.

Computer Searches. The computer databases that correspond to the ISI indexes (*Scisearch* and *Social Scisearch* in the Dialog system; see Chapter 9) can be searched in such a way that review articles are retrieved instantly. The searcher simply keys in the appropriate key words and then adds the specification "DT = REV 'OR' BIB" (i.e., Document Type equals Review or Bibliography). Many other databases in specialized fields (e.g., *MEDLINE, PSYCHINFO, ERIC*) have a similar "document type" feature that allows instant retrieval of review article citations. *This method is usually the fastest.*

ISI Indexes *(Science Citation Index, Social Sciences Citation Index, Arts & Humanities Citation Index).* The key word approach these provide can tell you which articles have been written on your subject; to find out if any of them is a review article, note how many footnotes the article has. The *SCI* will tell you how many footnotes each has; the *SSCI* and *A&HCI* will show you by listing them. Journal articles with large numbers of footnotes tend to be review articles.

Bibliographic Index (H. W. Wilson, 1937–). If your library doesn't own *ISR,* it may still have this basic Wilson index, which is a subject guide to published bibliographies, including those at the ends of journal articles. Its criterion for including a bibliography is that it must contain at least 50 citations. And so this *Index* is useful for finding review articles, since any journal article that has 50+ citations is likely to be a review. It also attempts to cover the various *Annual Review* type series systematically.

Library Literature (H. W. Wilson, 1933–). This index covers about 200 periodicals in the field of library science. It is useful for finding review-type articles because reference librarians often publish for each other annotated bibliographies or bibliographic essays that discuss all the best sources or finding aids on particular subjects (e.g., on criticisms of different novels; on "Women in religion," etc.) And often they are not picked up by *Bibliographic Index* because fewer than 50 sources are discussed. Unfortunately nobody *except* reference librarians uses these things, but they deserve a wider audience because they are first-rate starting points for research.

Modern Language Association and G. K. Hall Monographs. Review articles in the humanities are harder to find systematically than those in the sciences and social sciences, for they tend to be published as essays within books rather than as articles within journals. There are some in English literature, however, that interested students should know about. Most of them are published by the MLA and include: *The English Romantic Poets: A Review of Research and Criticism* (3rd rev. ed., ed. by Frank Jordan, 1972); *Victorian Prose: A Guide to Research* (ed. by David J. DeLaura, 1973); *Victorian Fiction: A Guide to Research* (ed. by George H. Ford, 1978); *The Victorian Poets: A Guide to Research* (ed. by Frederic E. Faverty; Harvard University Press, 1968); and *Anglo-Irish Literature: A Review of Research* (ed. by Richard J. Finneran, 1976). Each of these devotes a whole chapter to each of the major writers of the respective period, trying to synthesize all the scholarship that has been done. (Note that these are for specialists—they are not the best sources to which an undergraduate should turn for criticisms of particular literary works.) G. K. Hall publishes a more extensive collection of guides called the "Reference Guides to Literature Series." There are 120 titles in it, most providing a review article and a comprehensive bibliography of critical articles about a particular author in British or American literature. They are always cataloged under the heading "[Author's name]— Bibliography" in the card catalog. They also appear in *Bibliographic Index*.

The *Syntopicon* Index. This comprises volumes 2 and 3 of *Great Books of the Western World* (Encyclopaedia Britannica, 1952) and provides 102 review articles on philosophical subjects. For a shortcut, it should be used with Mortimer Adler and Charles van Doren's *Great Treasury of Western Thought* (Bowker, 1977), which provides in one volume the texts of many of the citations referred to in the *Syntopicon*, as documentation for the review articles. Various monographs from the Institute for Philosophical Research (e.g., on freedom, happiness, justice, love, progress) offer book-length reviews of philosophical thinking in similar areas.

Wilson Quarterly. This is one of the best sources of review articles written for laypeople who wish to keep informed about a wide variety of subjects; it is produced by the Woodrow Wilson International Center for Scholars at the Smithsonian Institution. Each issue presents a variety of articles on diverse fields that may range from public policy and social science issues to science, mathematics, religion, architecture, geography, history, art, or literature. Especially valuable regular features are its digests of significant articles from other journals in all fields and its summaries of important work done in elusive research reports. Each issue also includes a survey of current books as well. This one journal, in other words, draws together and reviews, synthesizes, and evaluates information that otherwise would escape the attention of even dedicated generalists. It is well written; it does not come out too frequently to make reading it cover to cover a chore; and it can save you the time and trouble of subscribing to many more journals. Subscription information is available in the *Standard Periodical Directory*.

Other sources that can often provide review-type information are the following:

- *Congressional hearings.* These are frequently overlooked by academic researchers, but they are a gold mine. Congressional investigations or oversight reviews extend into an amazing range of subject areas in the social sciences and sciences. (A recent estimate is that Congress holds an average of *37 hearings every day*.) And when Congress wants to find the best information on the current state of any situation, it generally gets it, for it calls the best experts available to testify. Moreover, hearings usually bring out all points of view on the subject at hand (although, of course, they *can* be manipulated for political purposes); and, further, Congress has the power of subpoena, a most useful investigative tool generally unavailable to other researchers. The best index to Congressional hearings since 1970 is the *CIS U.S. Congressional Index;* the same publisher has also produced another set called *CIS U.S. Congressional Committee Hearings through 1969,* which extends coverage all the way back to the early 1800s. Both indexes may be backed up by microfiche sets of the hearings themselves (see Chapter 12).

- *Congressional Committee Prints.* In addition to being able to draw on hearings for information, Congress can also use the Congressional Research Service of the Library of Congress, which often produces book-length "state-of-the-situation" reports on public policy issues. Many of these are published as committee prints. The best indexes to these are, again, the *CIS U.S. Congressional Index* for those since 1970; and the *CIS U.S. Congressional Committee Prints Index: From the Earliest Publications through 1969.* Libraries that own the indexes may also own microfiche sets of the prints.

- *Doctoral dissertations.* These are sometimes useful for review-type surveys, especially in areas of the humanities and social sciences—although the sciences are covered too—that don't get picked up by the *ISR* or the *Annual Review* type series. Frequently, writers will begin their dissertations with a survey of the literature of a field, in order to present a background and context for their own contribution to it. The best index is *Comprehensive Dissertation Index* (see Chapter 12).

- *Talking to knowledgeable people.* The human resources that lie outside the library's walls are often the best sources for overviews of a subject, as they can not only provide answers but also alert you to questions you didn't think of on your own (see Chapter 11).

Review articles located through any of the above print sources can often be updated by running them through the citation indexes to see if there has been any subsequent discussion of them.

To sum up the last four chapters on journal articles, several points are especially important:

- Subject heading access to journal articles is provided by the Wilson and Information Access indexes, and by hundreds of other indexes. The Wilson and Information Access sources use *Library of Congress Subject Headings* more or less closely.

- Key word searching allows you to find material that cannot be found through subject heading searches.

- Citation searching is still another valuable technique that will turn up additional material. The basic key word and citation sources are the three ISI indexes; but many others of both kinds exist as well.

- Review articles, like encyclopedia articles, are often excellent starting points for research.

8

Published Bibliographies

One of the best ways to start a research project is through subject bibliographies, which can be either published or computer-generated (the latter will be discussed in the next chapter). The published variety are especially important because they offer several advantages over their computerized cousins: they are compiled by human beings who can judge the relevance and importance of items; they often include nuggets that can be found only by serendipity and persistent searching in obscure sources not covered by databases; and they may include types of material and dates of coverage that are blind spots to computers. And in some cases they may provide a selective distillation of only the best materials to consider, chosen in light of a compiler's deep appreciation of a subject.

A bibliography can give you much more extensive and specific information than a card catalog; it can save you a great deal of browsing time; and it can list journal articles on a subject all in one place, so you don't have to repeat the same search through several different indexes and many annual volumes. It may also pick up "fugitive" sources such as dissertations, theses, pamphlets, and government documents that are not usually covered by most indexes. Further, it can alert you to the existence of relevant works not held by your local library, but which may still be available to you through interlibrary loan.

One of the most useful features of a published bibliography is that it will often allow you to do a simple "Boolean combination" search in records that are too old to be picked up by computer databases. This type of inquiry involves looking for two different subjects at the same time; and with databases such things are very easy to do. For example, I once helped a student who wanted to find a comparison of the educational philosophies of Aristotle and John Dewey. A search of a few databases with the command "select Aristotle and Dewey" turned up a list of recent works discussing both men. However, through a published bibliography we could do a similar search for older material not in the online files. Very simply, we consulted Milton Thomas's *John Dewey: A Centennial Bibliography* (University of Chicago Press, 1962; 370 pages); this is an exhaustive list of studies about Dewey. In looking at its index, under "Aristotle," we were immediately led to a number of works that discussed the two, some of which had not appeared on the printout.

Similarly, another student looking for studies of "Social Darwinism in the works of Thomas Hardy" could combine the two topics ("Darwinism" and "Hardy") by looking in the index to Helmut Gerber's *Thomas Hardy: An Annotated Bibliography of Writings About Him* (Northern Illinois University Press, 1973; 841 pages). The entry "Darwinism" led him to four citations in the list that proved to be directly relevant.

One problem that keeps coming up in research is that there is often no subject heading that is a good match for one's specific interest. Traditionally, libraries have offered two major avenues for circumventing this difficulty: systematic browsing of the subject-grouped books themselves in the classification scheme, and detailed subject bibliographies. The latter allow for very easy browsing of titles, and sometimes of annotations as well, that are free of the constraints of an artificial controlled vocabulary. The newer approaches (through key words, footnote citations, and "post-coordinate" combinations via computer) are the result of relatively recent advances in the technology of indexing; but they have merely supplemented rather than replaced the traditional methods. Published bibliographies will never be replaced by machine searches because, as mentioned before, they often reach materials that human compilers can find but that lie beyond the reach of databases. And, further, a printout is generated only in response to specific words being typed in, whereas a published list is compiled according to the ideas in a human mind without rigid verbal criteria of exclusion. Published bibliographies, in other words, can often present perspectives on the literature of a subject that cannot be duplicated by machine searches. And the published lists will continue to be valuable in any event because they provide the best access to records dating to the period before the advent of database coverage.

The main advantage of a bibliography is that it can save you the trouble of "re-inventing the wheel"—of doing the laborious spade work of identifying relevant sources. The disadvantage is that its compiler will almost never tell you how he or she compiled it or what sources were used—you won't know what was missed, in other words. Researchers pursuing a subject in depth can never rely on any one source to be completely exhaustive—in-depth research always requires a combination of various approaches and sources. For many projects, however, a good bibliography may be fully adequate.

There are several ways to find out if a published bibliography exists on a subject. Researchers should keep in mind the following:

The Card Catalog.   Four forms of subject headings in the Library of Congress system are relevant. After you have determined the proper word or phrase for your topic (or the one that comes closest) through the *LCSH* list, plug it into the following forms:

[Subject heading]—Bibliography
[Subject heading]—[Geographic subdivision]—Bibliography
Bibliography—Bibliography—[Subject heading]
Bibliography—Best books—[Subject heading]

Although the fourth looks to be the most promising, it is seldom and inconsistently used. The first two will always be your best bets.

A catalog card (or its electronic equivalent in a database) will usually note the presence of a bibliography at the end of a book, citing the specific pages on which it appears, which will tip you off to its length. And such a note can appear on any card under any subject heading. So even if you don't find the form "[Subject heading]—Bibliography," you may still be able to pick out bibliographies of several pages' length under other headings without the specific subdivision (Fig. 5).

Bibliographic Index (H. W. Wilson, 1937–). This is a very useful source, as it lists not only bibliographies that are separately

MONITOR (IRONCLAD)

E473
.2   **Hoehling, Adolph A**
.H57   Thunder at Hampton Roads / by A. A. Hoehling. — Engle-
       wood Cliffs, N.J. : Prentice-Hall, c1976.

       xvi, 231 p., [8] leaves of plates : ill. ; 24 cm.

       ➤ Bibliography: p. 221-[226]
       Includes index.
       ISBN 0-13-920652-3 : $9.95

       1. Hampton Roads, Battle of, 1862.   2. Monitor (Ironclad)   3. Shipwrecks
—North Carolina—Hatteras, Cape.   4. Hatteras, Cape—History.   5. Underwa-
ter archaeology.   I. Title.

       E473.2.H57   973.7'52   76-18261
                                                       MARC

       Library of Congress   76   MCat

Fig. 5

published, but also those that appear at the ends of books and journal
articles. Those that are included contain at least 50 citations, in English and foreign languages. The editors currently examine over 3000
periodicals in addition to books and annual publications, so its coverage is excellent. (In 1985, for example, 6675 monographs and 3325
serials were covered.) The subject headings it uses tend to be those of
the *LCSH* system.

A word to the wise, however: since this index covers a half-century
of publishing, it may list many bibliographies on your subject without
indicating their quality. To prevent information overload it may be
best, therefore, to first ask for help at the reference desk. I once helped
a student who wanted to find a bibliography on "Jacksonian democ-
racy," but she didn't ask for this—she just asked for the *Bibliographic
Index*. When I found out what she really wanted, however, I could
refer her directly to the *Harvard Guide to American History* and the
*Library of Congress Guide to the Study of the United States of Amer-
ica,* both of which provide excellent lists of books on this subject—
lists determined by standards of quality, not quantity of citations. Often
a librarian can short-circuit a potentially lengthy search in this way—
but you won't know unless you ask for help in the first place.

Encyclopedia Articles.   The bibliographies at the ends of these are very good for listing the standard or most highly recommended works on a subject; but they are usually very brief, and do not include specialized or narrowly focused works (e.g., they would not be good for someone looking for material on "Social Darwinism in Hardy"). Remember to look particularly for specialized encyclopedias (see Chapter 1).

Review Articles.   These have excellent and lengthy bibliographies, and can be located by the approaches discussed in Chapter 7.

Government Printing Office *Subject Bibliography Series*.   The federal government publishes material on an astonishing variety of subjects, and the over 250 subject bibliographies published by the GPO are the best shortcut to what is available. A free list of all topics covered can be obtained from the GPO (see Chapter 12).

Subject Guide to Books in Print.   This is a good shortcut that reference librarians use to find the most recent books on any subject. The *BPR (Book Publishing Record) Annual Cumulative* is even better for many searches. The subject index to *Paperbound Books in Print* and the *Subject Guide to Forthcoming Books* are also useful for identifying the most recent material. (The caveat to be observed here is that recency is not necessarily synonymous with quality.)

Theodore Besterman's *World Bibliography of Bibliographies* (4th ed., 5 vols.; Societas Bibliographica, 1965–1966).   This venerable source can be very useful for research in older literature. It is arranged by subject, listing thousands of published bibliographies. Volume 5 is a detailed index. An update is provided by Alice F. Toomey's *World Bibliography of Bibliographies 1964–1974* (2 vols., Rowman and Littlefield, 1977). As useful as the *World Bibliography* is on occasion, it is the observation of reference librarians that whenever a graduate students asks for "Besterman" without *also* asking for Toomey and the *Bibliographic Index*, then that student is probably being taught by a professor who is simply teaching from his or her own antiquated graduate notes.

Bonnie R. Nelson's *Guide to Published Library Catalogs* (Scarecrow, 1982).   There are hundreds of libraries that have specialized in acquiring materials in particular subject fields. Over 400 of these have published their catalogs, and each is a gold mine of sources in its area because such catalogs often provide in-depth indexing of individual journal articles, research reports, and chapters of books. Nelson's *Guide* is the best list of what is available; she describes each catalog in detail, and provides a good subject index.

Library Literature (H. W. Wilson Co., 1921– ; bimonthly with annual cumulations). This is a subject index to over two hundred library journals. It is surprisingly useful for bibliographies in *all* subject areas, however, because reference librarians use these journals to communicate with each other and to publish annotated lists of sources on things they get asked about. (For example, one of the journals, *Reference Service Review,* published in one recent issue three excellent bibliographies on how to get grant money, on field guides to birds, and on Afro-American movies.) And many of these articles are overlooked by *Bibliographic Index* because they contain fewer than 50 sources.

Serial Bibliographies. These are bibliographies covering particular topics that are published regularly, usually in specialized journals. Three good sources for identifying serial bibliographies are Richard Gray's *Serial Bibliographies in the Humanities and Social Sciences* (Pierian Press, 1969), William Wortman's *Guide to Serial Bibliographies for Modern Literatures* (Modern Language Association, 1982), and David Henige's *Serial Bibliographies and Abstracts in History* (Greenwood Press, 1986). *Bibliographic Index* is also useful for identifying the serials.

Related to the bibliography is another form of research aid called the "Guide to the Literature." This is ideally more than just a list of sources (with or without annotations); it frequently provides a running evaluative commentary on the literature of a subject, with full paragraphs in connected exposition. The better ones will discuss not only the finding aids and research techniques that are appropriate to the discipline, but also the basic and advanced works essential to the content of the field of study. They seek to convey a structure of perception for the field—which is more than a bibliography provides.

Some guides are more successful than others in achieving this ideal. *Sources of Information in the Social Sciences,* edited by William H. Webb (American Library Association, 1986), is a good example of what can be done. It should be read—not just referred to—by all researchers in the fields of history, geography, economics, sociology, anthropology, psychology, education, and political science. Others, such as Harold Kolb's *Field Guide for the Study of American Literature,* are little more than annotated lists of books. The word "Guide" in the title is no guarantee that the book is more than a bibliography of finding aids.

The following brief list of titles will suggest some of the variety of specialized guides—of varying quality—that are available:

> *A Brief Guide to Sources of Scientific and Technical Information*
> *Guide to English and American Literature*
> *The Reader's Advisor* (covering English, American, and world literature)
> *A Reader's Guide to the Social Sciences*
> *Guide to the Literature of Art History*
> *Guide to the Literature of the Life Sciences*
> *Guide to the Study of the United States of America* (and *Supplement*)
> *Harvard Guide to American History*
> *The Historian's Handbook*
> *How to Find Out in Philosophy and Psychology*
> *Research Guide to Musicology*
> *Research Guide to Philosophy*
> *Research Guide to Religious Studies*
> *Research Guide to the History of Western Art*
> *The Information Sources of Political Science*
> *Introduction to Library Research in French Literature*
> *Science and Technology: An Introduction to the Literature*
> *Guide to Sources for Agricultural and Biological Research*
> *The Use of Biological Literature*
> *The Use of Chemical Literature*
> *The Use of Medical Literature*

Usually such works can be found in the card catalog (or other sources using the *LCSH* system) under the form already mentioned, "[Subject heading]—Bibliography."

I mentioned that published bibliographies are often the best means of gaining access to literature too old to be in databases; they are *especially* useful for getting into pre-twentieth century literature, i.e., material written prior to the existence of even the printed indexes and card catalogs that we also take for granted today.

It is particularly useful to look for published bibliographies *in addition to* computer-generated lists. The bibliographies will almost always turn up valuable sources—*recent as well as old*—missed by the printouts. And it is important to *actively search* for such bibliographies. Almost every researcher has had the experience of using a bibliography that appears at the end of a book or article; but it is comparatively rare—at least from this reference librarian's perspective—for researchers to *start out* by looking for a published bibliography, as opposed to simply using one that happens to come their way as a by-product of something else they've done. A hallmark of the experts is that they actively look for such lists, and especially that they do so in the early stages of their investigations.

9

Computer Searches

Computer searches offer a convenient way to generate a bibliography on virtually any subject a researcher may be interested in, and they can provide other information as well. Basically, there are four kinds of online searches, and they should not be confused with each other:

1. OCLC-type searches, which serve as book or journal location devices (i.e., they can tell you which libraries in the country own a copy of the work you are seeking).

2. Searches through commercial systems (e.g., Dialog, SDC, BRS) that produce printouts of bibliographic citations on any subject, often with abstracts.

3. Searches using the online catalogs of particular libraries, which provide bibliographic citations to some materials (usually only recent books) held by those institutions.

4. Full-text searches, available through commercial systems, which retrieve whole articles, reports, or tabular data rather than just citations to them.

There are so many developments in the computer field, and they are happening so quickly, that only a fool would try to present a coherent overview of the situation. Let me begin with book-location databases.

OCLC-Type Searches

OCLC, Inc., is a shared-cataloging network with about 3800 participating libraries, with an additional 2500 adjunct members, in all 50 states, Canada, and several other countries. (The initials used to stand for "Ohio College Library Center"; but now, under different management, it is the "Online Computer Library Center.") Before the advent of this system (and others like it), individual libraries each had to do a considerable amount of original cataloging of new books to create catalog cards and other records of their holdings. Now, a library can find out if any other library in the system has already cataloged a particular book and use that information in the computer to generate the needed records for local use at the push of a button. Participants in the system do not have to individually re-invent the wheel for every new book, in other words.

The process of simplifying the task of cataloging produces a spin-off benefit: whenever a library uses the stored cataloging information on a particular book or journal, that library is automatically recorded by the system as owning that item. Searchers may therefore request the cataloging data on a book and then see a list of libraries that actually own a copy of the volume.

The operation started in 1967 but did not really attract a lot of members until the early 1970s, and so the database contains only records of works cataloged after these dates. Some libraries are going back and entering their earlier holdings into the system; but this is a very expensive operation and, under the present economic circumstances, there is little incentive to recatalog works for which they already have the necessary records, albeit in manual form. Still, there are hundreds of thousands of pre-1970 works in the database because even though they may have been published 50—or 350—years ago, they were not acquired and cataloged by a library until the last few years. And the date of the book's being cataloged, not that of its publication, determines its presence or absence in the database. Currently, the system records locations for about eleven million items, about a third of which were published prior to the 1960s.

Records in OCLC cannot be searched by subject—you must already know the author or the title of a work in order to find it.

There are two other networks in the United States that compete with OCLC. These are the Research Libraries Information Network (RLIN) and the Western Library Network (WLN). (A third system, UTLAS, links Canadian libraries but is seeking customers in the states as well.) RLIN includes several big-name libraries such as the New York Public, Yale, Princeton, Columbia, and Stanford; WLN is made up of libraries mainly in the Pacific Northwest. If a desired item cannot be located through an OCLC search, or through the several other sources discussed in Chapter 10, a search of RLIN or WLN may still turn up a copy. The RLIN database has an especially important feature: it is in the process of assembling catalog records, with library locations, for all works published anywhere in the entire British Empire in the eighteenth century, plus all works in English published anywhere else in the world for the same century. This is known as the Eighteenth Century Short Title Catalog project, and a huge set of microfiche of all the significant works identified in the project is also being produced, which is commercially available to research libraries.

Commercial Bibliographic Databases

Three major vendor companies provide the computer search services to which most libraries subscribe: Dialog Information Services, Inc. (a subsidiary of Lockheed Corp.), System Development Corporation (or SDC, which offers a search service known as ORBIT), and Bibliographic Retrieval Services (or BRS). A fourth source, the National Library of Medicine, offers its own MEDLARS system to subscribers; this is confined to medical and related subject areas, however.

The other three companies offer over 300 different databases. Each such database is a file of information (usually bibliographic citations to journal articles or research reports) in a particular subject area, stored in machine-readable form. There is considerable overlap in the files offered by the various vendors (e.g., the *Psychological Abstracts* database is offered by all three), but the broadest range is provided by Dialog. When the librarian or other trained searcher uses a local terminal connected via telephone line to the vendor's computer, he or she can interact with the machine to tailor the search to particular subjects or combinations of subjects. The methods of instructing the computer vary to some extent depending on which vendor's system is being used.

A computer search enables you to scan thousands of citations to journal articles in virtually any subject area. The result, in most cases, will be a printed bibliography tailored to your specific requirements; in some subject areas you have the option of receiving abstracts of the articles. Most searches done at academic libraries for students or other university personnel will probably cost between $5 and $30 for each database searched; this will include charges for the amount of computer and teleconnect time and for the number of citations actually retrieved. There may also be a surcharge for service levied by the individual library. Those who are not affiliated with a university can obtain searches through private research companies, through some local public libraries, or, sometimes, through joining a university library's "Friends of the Library" organization. Two good directories that list facilities that will do searches for you are the *Online Database Search Services Directory* (Gale Research) or any edition of *American Library Directory* after 1982. Both are likely to be in any public library.

The bibliography created by the computer will be mailed to the requesting library or search service and received about a week after the search is run; it can also be printed immediately at the local terminal if instant results are required, but this costs more in computer time and teleconnect fees. Most people wait for mail delivery if the printout will be lengthy.

The librarian or other searcher must select in advance which of the 300+ databases she wishes to search for your subject, and for some topics she may have to use several files. There is no way to search all of the databases simultaneously. The Dialog system, however, offers a separate "Dialindex" database that can efficiently point out which of the many files will yield results for a particular search statement. SDC and BRS have somewhat similar features.

People who request computer searches are well advised to be aware that many databases are in a one-to-one correspondence with a conventional printed index. The *Sociological Abstracts* computer file, for example, contains exactly the same information that can be found in the printed index of the same name. The education database, called *ERIC*, contains the same information as the printed version; similarly,

Historical Abstracts corresponds to its printed form, *Philosopher's Index* to its, and so on. The reason for this is that the computer companies simply acquire the magnetic tapes from which the printed indexes are originally generated and mount them in a way that allows for direct searching. In many cases, then, researchers who inquire about online services find that they really do not need them, and that a half hour spent with the print indexes is quite sufficient.

Often there are significant differences between the databases and the print indexes, however. In most instances only the comparatively recent years of an index are searchable online. The hard copy version of *Biological Abstracts,* for example, covers from 1927 to date; but only the years 1969 to the present are in the database. Similarly, the print index *Public Affairs Information Service (P.A.I.S.)* covers from 1915 to date; but only the years from 1976 are loaded in the computer. *Psychological Abstracts* is searchable online from 1967 onwards; but the hard copy version extends back to 1927.

There may be other differences as well. One can search titles and abstracts of doctoral dissertations via computer from June 1980 to date; but prior to that time one can search only their titles and not their abstracts, which were not put into the database. To search the abstracts, one must use the printed *Dissertation Abstracts.* Similarly, even though the *Biological Abstracts* database covers from 1969 to date, none of the entries from 1969 through June 1976 includes an abstract.

The scope of coverage (as well as the dates) may also vary between print and online versions. Since May 1980 the *Psychological Abstracts* database has included about 25% *more* material (mainly doctoral dissertations) than is found in the print version. And, on the other side of the coin, the computer files corresponding to the *Science* and *Social Sciences Citation Index*es, for several years of coverage, have *less* material than their printed counterparts:

- The hard copy *Science Citation Index* (1955–   ) covers conference proceedings and multiauthored books and *Festschriften* (indexed at the chapter or essay level) for five years, 1977–1981, in addition to its coverage of journal articles and "Annual Review" type publications. But the corresponding *Scisearch* database (1974–   ) includes only the latter forms—not the conference proceedings or multiauthored books. But as of 1982 the two are essentially the same again (neither covering the proceedings or multiauthored books), although *Scisearch* covers *Current Contents,* which the print version does not.

- The hard copy *Social Sciences Citation Index* (1966–   ) covers multiauthored anthologies indexed at the chapter or essay level, in addition to journals, for the years 1979–1982. It also covers conference proceedings for the three years 1979–1981. The *Social Scisearch* database (1972–   ), however, covers only journals.

As might be expected, there are both advantages and disadvantages in having a computer search done rather than using the print indexes. There are several advantages:

1. The computer can save you time in searching. When you use print indexes, you have to repeat the same search over and over again through many annual volumes and monthly supplements—some of which may be missing from the shelf in your particular library. But the machine can search all the information within a database all at once.

2. The computer may be slightly more up-to-date than the print index. The newest "issue" of an index may be loaded online days or even weeks before the print version appears on the library's shelves.

3. In addition to searching subject headings, the computer can search for key words within titles or even abstracts. This is an extremely important advantage, especially in those files for which the print version allows access only through a controlled-vocabulary system. *Psychological Abstracts,* for instance, has its own controlled-vocabulary list of subject headings, so you must find a relevant term from this list in order to gain subject access to the printed version of the index. This can be a problem if there is no term in the list that corresponds to what you want. To return to a previous example, a researcher at the time of the Iranian hostage crisis had trouble in this regard, since in 1980 there were no subject headings using the words "Hostage," "Captive," "Terrorism," or "Kidnap"; nor were variants such as "Captivity" or "Terrorist" used. Nor were there any cross-references from these words to other terms that were acceptable to the system. In using the print index, then, he was stymied. But in having a computer search done he circumvented the difficulty because the machine was able to examine the same file of information for *any* word appearing in either the titles or the abstracts; and a search on the terms "hostage?" or "terror?"[1] produced a large list of directly relevant articles.

(The records on a computer printout have a "descriptor field" analogous to the subject tracings on a catalog card, which told the searcher in this case that the articles did indeed appear in the print index—under the headings "Violence" and "Crime victims.") Similarly, a few years ago the same *Psychological Abstracts* thesaurus did not have the term "Burnout" as either a heading or a cross-reference; but a computer search under the term as a key word produced a bibliography of over two hundred items. And here the descriptor fields indicated that the articles were scattered under several subject headings in the print index (e.g., "Employee attitudes," "Occupational adjustment," "Occupational aspirations," "Occupational stress"). Here, a key word approach was clearly more efficient than that afforded by subject headings.

Academic researchers in the fields of language, literature, and linguistics should especially note that the Modern Language Association's *MLA International Bibliography* is searchable online, although at present only from the 1960s to date. (The entire index from 1921 will eventually be entered into the database.) The print version of this index, prior to 1981, is notoriously difficult to search for subjects other than particular authors and their works. The computer, however, now provides key word access to any terms within the titles of books or articles.

4. In some databases the machine can also do other types of searches that are not possible with the printed indexes, such as searching by document type. In the general *Scisearch* and *Social Scisearch* files, for example, one can search directly for state-of-the-art review articles. And many of the other databases that are more comprehensive in specialized fields (e.g., *PSYCHINFO, ERIC, MEDLINE*) have similar features that can pull out review articles, or letters to the editor, or book reviews, curriculum guides, and so on.

5. Another major advantage of a computer search is its ability to look for two or more subject terms at the same time. For example, if you are interested in "Fungal diseases in conifers in Canadian forests," in a printed index you would have to look under at least three different headings (fungal diseases, conifers, Canada) separately, and then weed out all the articles that don't appear under each of the three. But the computer can search all three subjects simultaneously and give you only the citations that meet all three specifications.

This combining or crossing capability is particularly useful where each separate idea is itself expressable in several variant phrasings. For example, one researcher was interested in articles on "Computer-assisted instructional techniques in the field of geography." In looking through the subject heading list for the major database in the field of education, called *ERIC*, he found that several descriptors were useful to express each of the two ideas he wanted to combine:

Programed instruction	Geography
Learning laboratories	Physical geography
Programed instructional materials	World geography
	Geography instruction
Computer-assisted instruction	Geographic concepts

A search of the corresponding printed *ERIC* indexes under all nine headings would have been very time consuming. The computer, however, could search for all four of the first-column terms at once, and all five of the second column, and then cross the two sets against each other, printing only those citations that "hit" at least one descriptor from each column simultaneously. Had he so desired, the searcher could have introduced a third column, limiting the output to only those citations indexed under the descriptors "Secondary schools," "Secondary education," "Secondary school curriculum," and so on. A further specification could have produced a final set composed only of those relevant articles published in the last five years.

The computer accomplishes this process of combining and screening through operations of "Boolean logic,"[2] which can be illustrated in Figure 6a. If Circle A represents the set of citations retrieved by terms expressing one subject idea (either controlled-vocabulary descriptors or key words or both), and Circle B represents another subject, then the area of overlap represents those citations that deal with both subjects. Other circles or limiting factors can be introduced for further specification. And other types of combinations are possible, as shown in Figure 6b and 6c.

The combination of these five factors frequently makes computer searching a highly useful technique. There are, however, some limitations to its usefulness; and there are positive disadvantages as well:

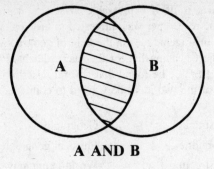

A AND B

a.

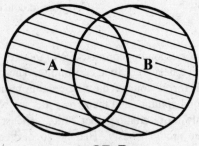

A OR B

b.

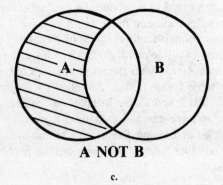

A NOT B

c.

Fig. 6

1. A computer search costs money, and the bibliography it generates takes time to arrive. Usually the printout will be received in less than a week; but it still takes a matter of days. (Those researchers who want an instant printout can obtain it at the local terminal, but this will cost more.) For brief or uncomplicated searches, the use of print indexes rather than their online versions can thus save both time and money.

2. Contrary to the naive assumption held by many people, the computer cannot tap into "all knowledge." Nor can it search all of its 300+ databases simultaneously—each must be selected and entered separately. Moreover, the vocabulary used to search one file may not work in the others—the subject terms may have to be tailored to each. And without such careful tailoring you may miss the best material.

3. The databases are mainly good for picking up journal articles and research reports. Some of them, particularly within the last few years, are picking up books, too—but the problem is that you cannot *count* on them to have picked up all relevant monographs. The various producers of the files publish lists of the journals they index; but they don't do this for books, nor do they clearly specify the criteria by which they select books. A further problem relates to the depth of indexing done on monographs—do they index the contents of individual chapters? Or of the book as a whole? Or just title key words? The indexing procedures are seldom clear.

4. The number of descriptors or subject headings assigned to each article may vary greatly from one database to the next. *Historical Abstracts* averages 3.6 per article; *Psychological Abstracts,* 6; and *NTIS* (National Technical Information Service) between 8 and 24. The number of these assigned points of access determines how readily the information can be retrieved and how successfully Boolean combinations will work. And even in those databases in which access is only through key words, the number of words available for each item determines its accessibility—that is, if you can search only titles, you cannot retrieve as many items as you could if abstracts were also searchable. Most dissertations, for example, are retrievable only through title key words, since abstracts are not in the database prior to June 1980.

The type of problem this results in is illustrated by the student of English literature who wishes to compile a list of all doctoral dissertations on the Romantic critic and essayist William Hazlitt. A computer search on "Hazlitt?" in the *Dissertation Abstracts* database turns up over 50 items—but it also misses *at least a dozen* other dissertations having substantial sections on the essayist. The reason is that these extra items pre-date 1980 and do not use the essayist's name in their titles, among which are *The Romantic Critics' Opinions of Elizabethan Non-Dramatic Literature* and *English Prose of the Romantic Age: The Matter of Style*.[3]

5. Another related problem has to do with the difficulty of thinking up all synonyms and variant phrasings for a subject. For example, I once did a search on "women in the armed forces" in the *Social Scisearch* database, looking for title key words. I initially searched for "women" crossed against these terms:

army?
navy?
air forc?
marines?
service academ?
combat?
battle?
soldier?
armed force?

The result was a printout of 36 citations. I then noticed that I had forgotten to include the word "military?"; and a search on this, crossed against "women?" turned up *18 additional* articles (i.e., after the overlap with the previous 36 had been eliminated).

Similarly, a searcher looking for material on "parental grief on the death of a child" must remember to search not only "parent?" but also "mother?," "father?," "maternal," and "paternal." And in other key word searches, "fourth" and "4th" must both be specified, as well as "color" and its British spelling "colour." In a database that does not have a controlled vocabulary system to round up variant phrasings, such problems are numerous. And this points up a *major disadvantage* of a computer search: *it will give you exactly what you ask for and nothing more.* (And even in controlled-vocabulary files you have to specify *all* the relevant descriptors; and there may be no cross-references online.) It is like an extremely efficient idiot. You cannot casually browse through all the citations in the database because to see any of them you must specify in advance what you want to see. And if your specification is even slightly off, you may miss a very important group of citations. When you use a print index, on the other hand, you have a *major advantage* in exactly the area where the computer is weak: you can *recognize* relevant items that you weren't specifically looking for. You can *browse*. Those researchers who supplement a computer search with a quick manual "once over" of the corresponding print index sometimes turn up additional citations—or additional terms to type into the online file—especially if it is a key word index.

6. As noted above, most of the databases contain citations only from about the late 1960s or early 1970s, while the corresponding print indexes may cover many decades. When librarians point this out to students, however, the response we get is almost invariably, "Oh well, I need only the most recent material anyway." The facile assumption implied here is that the most recent material will always cite or recapitulate anything of value from the older material. But there is a good chance that it won't—especially since many recent articles have themselves been researched solely on the basis of other computer searches. It is very easy for a vicious circle to develop—one in which researchers unwittingly rely too heavily on recent sources that have themselves relied too heavily on only recent sources. Human thought and scholarship did not begin only in the late 1960s. You must be careful not to let your research be shaped too much by the simple convenience of one particular tool of research; the material that is most easily retrievable is not necessarily or automatically the best, most insightful, or most important.

7. When you have a computer search done, you are to some extent relinquishing to another person the responsibility for your research. And you have no guarantee that the searcher will do everything that you would want. For example, I was once asked to do a search for a graduate student in sociology on the topic "blended families" or "stepfamilies" (i.e., those in which a parent remarries, resulting in a new family with stepchildren and a stepparent). The student assured me that she was already familiar with much of the literature, that she had checked through several annual volumes of the print indexes, and that she was sure that these two terms were the only ones being used. I therefore did a search using these terms, in three databases, and I came up with fifteen items. But I also noticed that the abstracts of

some of the citations were using the term "reconstituted families." And so I went back and searched the three files again using this new term and I found *nineteen additional* items that had not been retrieved in the first search.

The question is obvious: what would have happened if I hadn't noticed the additional term? The answer is that the student would have missed more than half of the works she wanted to see—and she probably would never have known it. Since most people are very naive about what a computer printout actually covers, it is likely that she would have assumed that she had "everything" on her subject.

How often are searchers guilty of such potential omissions? It's hard to say because the only mistakes we can talk about are the ones we almost made, but caught. I suspect that if you had five different searchers look for information on the same subject, you would probably have as many different printouts. It is to be hoped that there would be considerable overlap in the results; but I would be surprised if the five were identical. Much depends on how successfully the searcher manages the initial interview with the requester, and there is considerable room for variation here. In other words, one computer search is *by no means* necessarily as good as another—*who* does the search for you is a big factor in determining *what* you will get for results. If you are associated with an academic institution, one good way to find out the names of the best searchers to to ask the student assistants in the reference department. They usually know who is most capable.

8. Computer searches on key words are likely to produce some— or many—citations that have the right words in the wrong context. A search of the words "President" and "Washington" will turn up articles on George Washington—but also material on the President of Washington College. A search for material on the history of steamboats once turned up an article on the similarity of birth defects in five babies in Steamboat Springs, Colorado. A (bad) search that was intended to retrieve articles on "how labor supply in an area affects managerial decisions on locating plants" crossed "labor" and "manag?" and unwittingly retrieved hundreds of articles on labor-management relations.

In such cases the computer cannot distinguish meaningful contexts; it can only find the words you have instructed it to find. To oversimply a bit, if you tell the machine to locate articles on "Venetian blinds," it will do so—but it may also find articles on "blind Venetians." A mechanically produced bibliography can have many irrelevancies that would not be found in a list produced by a human being who has actually read and evaluated the items he includes. And on a printout every irrelevant item costs just as much as one that is on target; you have to pay for all of them.

Computer searches thus have both advantages *and disadvantages*. To use them intelligently you must recognize their limitations as well as their strengths. The important thing to remember is that they are only one weapon available to the researcher; they are not the whole arsenal. A thorough review of the literature of any subject requires a *combination* of the approaches discussed in this book.

Online Library Catalogs

Many academic and public libraries are now making a change from card catalogs to computers. In most cases the switch involves closing the manual file and beginning the coverage of the database from that point forward—that is, the computer will usually not pick up retro-spectively the material covered by the cards. In using an online cata-log, then, the first thing you must find out is its dates of coverage.

It is *especially* important not to confuse the coverage of an online library catalog with that of, say, a Dialog search. Commercial services such as Dialog include hundreds of databases that cover a very wide range of materials: books, journal articles, conference papers, disser-tations, government documents, research reports, and newspaper arti-cles. An online catalog search, however, is usually only *one* database of information on books—and only the books of the one library whose catalog is being searched. It will not list "everything" in the library, in other words; and yet a surprising number of people seem to think that any "computer search" is just as good as any other, and that "all knowledge" is somehow magically available through one-stop shop-ping at a library terminal. And what is just as frequent an occurrence is that even when librarians inform users of what is not covered by online catalogs, many of them still say that they will simply "settle for whatever is on the printout," as though the computer had auto-matically selected the best material. College students are the most fre-quent offenders in this regard; professors who expect high quality research should insist that their students use sources other than online catalogs alone.

In most cases the contents of such a catalog will be similar to that of the manual file it supersedes, that is, the individual items that can be searched will be the electronic equivalents of catalog cards, each containing the name of a book's author, its title, call number, and so on, and two or three subject headings. What is likely to be different are the number of access points to the same information. With cards you can search by author, title, or approved subject heading; but with computers you may be able to search, in addition, by key words appearing anywhere on the record, by call number, by date of publication, by series, by language, or by any combination of such entries. It used to be that libraries had to limit the number of access points in a manual catalog to only a few because each additional point required the creation and filing of an entirely separate card (e.g., if access by author is desired, one card for the book must be filed under the author's name; if access by two subject headings is desired, two separate cards must be created and filed). In a manual system, you cannot have access to a book under ten different subject headings without creating a very bulky and difficult-to-use file.

But with a computerized record you can have as many points of access as you want because all of them are on *one* record, the creation of which entails neither the labor and expense of making and filing multiple copies of the record, nor the space problems of a physically bulky file.

Libraries now have the opportunity to create catalog records that allow a much greater depth of access to information. Theoretically, the tables of contents or chapter headings of books can now be added to catalog records to provide many more points of subject access; it is also now possible to add more than just the traditional two or three subject headings. Few libraries are making full use of the new opportunities, however; most follow the lead of the Library of Congress, which continues to create computerized records with not much more than the old-fashioned minimum of information on them.

The fact that online catalogs are very "high tech" and that, often, they will provide you with a *free* printout of results makes them very attractive research tools. Again, however, you must be on guard not to let the scope of your research be channelled too much in one direction by the fact that one tool is more visible or more attractive than others. It is advisable to recall that an online catalog will probably *not* cover such sources as:

- Individual chapters of books.
- Journal and magazine articles.
- Newspaper articles.
- State-of-the-art review articles.
- Nonbook formats such as prints, posters, photographs, motion pictures, sound recordings, sheet music, maps, and manuscripts.
- Research reports such as those from the National Technical Information Service (NTIS; see Chapter 12) or the Educational Resources Information Center (ERIC).
- U.S. government documents.
- Microform research collections.

In other words, even if you do a good search in an online catalog, the likelihood is that you will be getting only the tip of the iceberg of what the library contains.

Full-Text Searches

Some companies offer databases that contain the full texts of newspaper or journal articles, court decisions, research reports, and so on, rather than just citations to them. Preeminent among these is the Mead Corporation, which produces the LEXIS and NEXIS databases. LEXIS is a huge resource in the field of law; it contains the full text of the United States Code plus full decisions from the Supreme Court, Courts of Appeal, District Courts, and Courts of Claims. It also provides specialized "libraries" in tax, securities, trade regulation, communications, labor, patent and copyright, and other law-related subjects. NEXIS is a similarly huge database containing the full texts of all the stories in major newspapers and wire services for at least three years back, plus all articles from major magazines for at least the last five years. It includes full coverage of the *Washington Post, New York Times, Newsweek,* and *U.S. News & World Report*—among ca. 350

other magazines—plus all Associated Press and United Press International releases.

An example of the extreme versatility of such databases is provided by a particular search once done at the State Department Library. The requester wanted background information about a candidate for a 90-day appointment, but all he had to go on was that the man had an unusual first name and a very common last name (as, say, "Dietrich Smith," although that is not the person's real name) and that he was from Peoria. A NEXIS search crossing "Dietrich" and "Peoria" was sufficient to retrieve an article that contained useful information.

The *Dow Jones News/Retrieval* service is another source of full-text material. It includes reports on individual companies, industries, stocks, bonds, financial matters in general, and events in the news (including sports, movie reviews, and weather reports).

Dialog is also getting more and more into the field of full-text databases. Among such files searchable on its system are:

- *Academic American Encyclopedia,* which contains 30,000 articles and tables on all subjects, including material not found in the printed edition.

- *AP News,* which provides all stories from the Associated Press DataStream service.

- *Commerce Business Daily,* which is the daily newsletter announcing and soliciting U.S. government contracts.

- *Harvard Business Review,* which provides the full text of the journal from 1976 to date, plus citations and abstracts for articles published from 1971 to 1975.

- *Magazine ASAP* and *Trade and Industry ASAP,* which provide complete texts of over 130 general and business magazines from January 1, 1983, to date.

- The full text of the King James version of the Bible.

Dialog offers over a dozen other full-text databases as well, primarily in the fields of business and current events. Others are planned for the future.

Despite the ongoing trend—indeed, rush—to put more full-text and tabular material online, it is worthwhile to remember that the bibliographic databases which provide only citations or abstracts rather than full texts will always allow you to do more extensive (although less in-depth) searches—and for a reason. Whenever a complete text is mounted, the database producer or vendor must have a licensing agreement with the owner of the copyright of the text. When citations *to* a text are offered, however, there are no copyright restrictions, and so coverage can be much broader.

These four different kinds of computer searches—book location, bibliographic citation, online library catalog, and full-text—are having an enormous impact on the way in which researchers operate. Especially valuable are their capabilities to search for key words in addition to subject headings and to do Boolean crossings of two or more subjects against each other. It should be noted, however, that computers are not the *only* means of finding such combinations of subjects. The extended list includes:

1. *Computer searches.*

2. *The Permuterm Subject Index* volumes of ISI indexes, which enable you to search for combinations of any two key words appearing in the titles of journal articles (see Chapter 5).

3. *Precoordinated subject headings in conventional indexes and catalogs.* With a computer you can take two or more subjects that have not already been combined and cross them against each other to determine if there is any area of overlap; this is known as post-coordination of subjects. A *pre*coordinated heading, on the other hand, is one that in effect has already done such a combination for you; it already expresses in one phrase the overlap of two or more subjects, so you don't have to put them together yourself through post-coordinating computer manipulations. Examples of such pre-coordinate headings in the *Library of Congress Subject Headings* system are:

> Women in aeronautics
> Sports for children
> Theatre in propaganda
> Minorities in medicine—United States—Mathematical models
> Education and heredity
> Doping in sports
> Smallpox in animals
> Television and children—South Africa

4. *Standard subdivisions limiting headings in conventional indexes and catalogs.* Rather than expressing a relationship of one subject to another, standard subdivisions were originally used to distinguish the various aspects that are *within* one subject. This distinction is usually nonexistent in actual cataloging practice, however. Their use constitutes another form of the precoordination of two or more terms. Examples in the *LCSH* system are:

> United States—History—Civil War, 1861–1865—
>   Regimental histories
> World War, 1939–1945—Underground movements—France
> Juvenile delinquency—Case studies
> Corporations—Charitable contributions
> Hospitals—Job descriptions
> Hardware—Marketing
> Cancer—Psychological aspects
> Flatulence—Anecdotes, facetiae, satire, etc.

There are hundreds of thousands of actual and potential precoordinated headings in any catalog or index that uses the *LCSH* vocabulary system; some other controlled vocabularies have analogous capabilities. Reference librarians are trained, literally, *to think in these terms*—and researchers who wish to exploit collections in the same way are well advised to study the booklet mentioned in Chapter 2, *Library of Congress Subject Headings: A Guide to Subdivision Practice* (LC, 1981). To the extent that you understand the possibilities and probabilities that there may be a precoordinated heading for your subjects, you can in effect do Boolean limitations without a computer. This is an especially important skill to have if you need to do research in material too old to be in a database that allows for post-coordination. (Overzealous computer buffs sometimes tend to suggest that combinations of subjects can be found *only* with computers, as though it never occurred to anyone before about 1968 to want to put two or more ideas together. The standard subdivisions in the *LCSH* system, however, allow for surprising range and flexibility in this regard.)

5. *Bibliographies with indexes.* This is sometimes the best way to cross ideas against each other. For example, a scholar looking for material comparing the philosophy of Sartre with that of Christianity could turn to Franics H. Lapointe's *Jean-Paul Sartre and His*

Critics: An Annotated Bibliography (1938–1980). He could then simply turn to its index to see which of the studies is listed under "Christianity." (There are eleven.)

Even if a subject bibliography does not have an index, it is usually only a matter of a few moments to scan through its entries to look for relevant titles. "Combinations" can thus also be accomplished by systematic browsing in bibliographies. This is a good technique to remember because post-coordination via computers does not always work. (Again, remember that *nothing* works *all the time*— you must therefore have a variety of approaches at your disposal.) *Published subject bibliographies are especially useful in allowing you to "cross" ideas in the older literature that is not picked up by databases.*

The versatility of computer searches is so dazzling that a large number of researchers are failing to note or heed their limitations. And, contrary to the popular saying, what you don't know *can* hurt you. I have seen this problem repeatedly, particularly with graduate students who want to do a literature review in preparation for writing a dissertation. One student, for example, told me that she'd heard that "there was a way to have all your research done for you automatically," and she wanted to know how to have that done. When I tried to explain to her how computer searches work, and that they have certain limitations as to what they can provide, she did not want to listen. She wanted a printout that would give her everything, period, and didn't care to hear otherwise. She finally said she'd "settle" for the computer search anyway, as she was "sure" it would give her enough for her dissertation (!) and, besides, she had a job and therefore "didn't have the time to do any other research." (This attitude is by no means atypical.) Never mind that she was missing single-author books, or relevant chapters or discussions within books, on her subject; never mind that she was missing journal articles written before the early 1970s; never mind that she was searching only a few key words from only the titles of previous doctoral dissertations. Her casual assumption, as found in so many students, was that only "the most recent" material is worth reading, and that the computer would give her "everything" she needed.

What is just as bad is that professors who direct doctoral dissertations *allow* computer searches to pass for complete literature reviews—for the professors are usually just as naive about their limitations as the students are.[4]

What this amounts to can only be described as cultural lobotomy on a grand scale. When a significant percentage of our most educated people (prospective Ph.D.s) relies almost exclusively on computer searches for "in-depth" research, then we are fostering the growth of an intellectual system with very shallow roots. Since so much of the written memory of humanity before the 1970s is not in the computer in the first place—or is only superficially indexed—it is likely to be ignored by immature scholars if it isn't as easily retrievable as the more recent material. The older material—especially the older journal articles—"does not compute"; and to many graduate students this tends as a practical matter to mean "therefore it is not important." There tends to be a similar neglect of certain forms of literature, especially single-author books, because machines more readily retrieve journal articles and research reports. A moment's reflection will indicate that the computers are no better than the material that is loaded into them; and yet a surprising number of researchers expect them to be omniscient.[5]

I suspect the major reason for this situation lies in the fact that professors continue to tell their students "You're no scholar if you can't find what you need by yourself." Librarians who teach "bibliographic instruction" classes often leave behind a similar crippling message. The result is that inadequately prepared students—who don't even know how to use the subject headings in a card catalog—feel that there is a stigma attached to them whenever they ask for help with anything *except* computer searches. (The latter have no stigma because even professors know that database searches require the intervention of a librarian. What they apparently do not know is how many other searches require a similar intervention.) The problem is compounded by those who teach "Methods of Research" or "Library Instruction" classes simply as a list of specific sources (e.g., *Readers' Guide*, Besterman's *World Bibliography of Bibliographies*). When a student cannot find what he needs from the list he's been given, and feels he'll be criticized if he asks for help of any sort other than that of requesting a computer search, then it is very easy for him to conclude that such searches are both necessary and sufficient. In other words, the very people who should know better are sometimes unwittingly encouraging students to follow the path of least resistance—and to the exclusion of other paths that would lead to additional, and very often better or more appropriate, material.

Still, the *appropriate* use of computers is a boon of tremendous value to researchers. Two questions that must arise, then, are "How can I find out which databases exist in my subject area?" and "How can I find out what limitations there are in the coverage of these databases?" Several directories provide this information:

- *Data Base Directory* (Knowledge Industry Publications and the American Society for Information Sciences; irregular), which covers 1800 files with an index by subject.

- *Computer-Readable Databases: A Directory and Data Sourcebook* (Knowledge Industry Publications, for the American Society for Information Sciences; biennial) which covers over 700 databases, with a subject index.

- *Online Bibliographic Databases: A Directory and Sourcebook* (Gale Research; revised irregularly), which covers about 180 files.

- *Encyclopedia of Information Systems and Services* (Gale Research; revised irregularly), which describes about 1500 databases and tells you whether the ones you want are available through the Dialog, SDC, or BRS systems, to which most libraries subscribe.

- *Datapro Complete Guide to Dial-Up Databases* (Datapro Research Corp.), a 600-page looseleaf directory of over 1400 databases with full descriptions and a subject index.

The major points to remember about computer searches are that they allow key word access to records otherwise available only through subject headings, and that they allow for post-coordinate Boolean combinations of two or more different subjects. Beyond this, it is important to be aware that online searches do *not* provide access to "everything" and that, in fact, they have distinct *disadvantages as well as advantages*—and that their ability to combine subjects can sometimes be matched or superseded by other, conventional approaches. Computers, in short, are a very powerful resource for researchers—but they are only one among many, and they are by no means always the best resource for particular inquiries.

Notes

1. The "?" symbol represents word truncation in the Dialog system. Thus "hostage?" will retrieve either "hostage" or its plural or possessive forms, "hostages," "hostage's," and so on. Similarly, "child?" will retrieve "child," "children," "child's," and "children's"—but also "childish," "childhood," "childbirth," and so on.

2. So named after George Boole (1815–1864), a British mathematician and logician who developed an analogy between the operations of logic and those of ordinary algebra.

3. Another of these "extra" dissertations is interesting for a different reason; it is John W. Crawford's *Romantic Criticism of Shakespearean Drama* (see *Dissertation Abstracts,* vol. 30A, no. 3, p. 1130). This is a discussion of many critics in the Romantic tradition, extending to the present, one of whom is Hazlitt. Students of Hazlitt would thus find it useful in supplying an overview of a tradition in which the essayist plays a significant part. The point of interest is that although Hazlitt is discussed in the dissertation, his name does not appear in its title *or even in its abstract.* Thus, even if all abstracts were available in the database, this relevant work would still have been missed by a "Hazlitt?" search.

4. In helping one reader at the Library of Congress's in-house Computer Catalog Center, I found that she was doing research for her professor on a subject that was not well covered by the database she was searching; I found, too, that she was also missing the few records that were available in it because she hadn't found the right subject headings to use. When I suggested that she might get better results with the conventional printed indexes, she replied that the professor wanted a *computer* search done, and that, besides, he was compiling only a "selected" bibliography for his publication. What is noteworthy is that the criterion of selection here was simply whatever came up on a printout produced by a searcher using the wrong database in the first place and searching it with the wrong terms. As ludicrous as this sounds, it is unfortunately not uncommon.

5. A similar expectation seems to exist in the field of medical diagnosis. Stanley J. Reiser observes in *Medicine and the Reign of Technology* (Cambridge, 1981) that physicians are slighting patients' own testimony of their symptoms, and physicians' observations and interpretations, in favor of the quantifiable, machine-produced data afforded by the latest medical technology, and that what is really needed is a balance of the three. The problems caused by overreliance on the machines for diagnosis is further discussed in the *Washington Post,* February 25, 1983, p. A8.

10

Locating Material in Other Libraries

If your own library does not own the specific source you need, or if you just want to know what is available elsewhere on your subject, you will want to look into the holdings of other libraries. There are three steps involved:

1. Determining which specific sources exist on your subject.
2. Determining where copies of these can be found.
3. Determining which libraries have special collections on your subject, for further research or browsing.

Determining Which Materials Exist on Your Subject

The best place to start is usually your own local public or university library. The footnotes and bibliographies in the books you've located through the card catalog and the classification scheme and the sources you've identified through the journal indexes, subject bibliographies, or databases may be enough to identify most of the best literature on your subject. Beyond these, however, there are several other good sources for identifying books in your area of interest; the most notable include *Book Review Digest* (with its subject index), *Subject Guide to Books in Print,* the *Cumulative Book Index,* the *BPR Annual Cumulative,* and the *Library of Congress Catalogs: Subject Catalog* (which is now continued as a part of the microfiche *National Union Catalog*). Each of these uses the *LC Subject Headings* list for its basic vocabulary control of subject terms.

Book Review Digest.   Given the avalanche of books that are available, most people will want to focus or limit their searches to a few works, at least initially. Two ways to do this are to limit either by quality of material or by recency of publication. And there are two good shortcuts to finding the quality books on a subject. One is to check several relevant encyclopedia articles to see if their selective bibliographies mention the same works. (It is particularly useful to compare a bibliography from a specialized encyclopedia with the one from the *Britannica;* the latter provides critical annotations to the entries in its bibliographies, which the other encyclopedias do not.) The purpose of an encyclopedia article is to give you a basic orientation to its subject, and so its bibliography will usually try to list only the most important works. And writers of encyclopedia articles are usually experts in their fields, so by comparing the views of two or more experts on what the important books are, you can often short-circuit some otherwise lengthy research. The second shortcut is to use *Book Review Digest* (H. W. Wilson, 1905–   ). This monthly publication has annual cumulations that form a permanent set; it covers reviews appearing in 70 American, British, and Canadian journals to about 6000 books every year. The important things about *BRD* are that it provides digests or extended quotations from several evaluative reviews of each book so that you can assess its critical reception from several viewpoints; and that it has a subject index. If you start with this index, you can quickly find citations to relevant books *and* an assessment of their quality. And this works with both recent and older sources. It is sometimes advisable to use this source in addition to the encyclopedia bibliographies, especially if these are somewhat dated.

Subject Guide to Books in Print.   This is an annual set listing those works published in the United States that are currently available in bookstores or by mail. It quotes prices; and a companion set, *Title Guide to Books In Print* (there's also an *Author Guide*) gives publishers' addresses. *Subject Guide* provides an efficient way to identify the most recent books on a subject. Its LC headings are rather broad (i.e., it makes little use of the standard subdivisions to limit topics), so you will have to do some browsing for specific works. And there are companion volumes you will also want to check: *Books in Print Supplement, Subject Guide to Forthcoming Books,* and *Paperbound Books in Print* (which has its own subject index). All libraries will own all of these volumes, and will usually have them right next to each other in the reference department.

Cumulative Book Index (or *CBI;* H. W. Wilson, 1928–). This is a monthly publication with annual cumulations. Unlike *Books in Print,* which is limited to works published in the United States, the *CBI* is an ongoing record of all English language books published anywhere in the world. It lists each under author, title, and subject entries, all interfiled in one alphabetical sequence.

BPR Annual Cumulative. *BPR* is the yearly hardbound cumulation of the monthly publication *American Book Publishing Record.* It is a list of books published in the United States, but it has three advantages over *Subject Guide to Books in Print:* (1) it lists entries in subject groupings according to the Dewey Decimal Classification, which greatly facilitates browsing; (2) its subject index uses *LCSH* terms *with* the subdivisions usually omitted in *Subject Guide,* and these are very useful for fine-tuning a search or combining two or more subjects; and (3) its entries give the tracings for each book, which are very useful for suggesting related subject headings. There are large cumulations for 1876–1949, 1950–1977, and 1980–1984, with annuals thereafter.

Library of Congress Catalogs: Subject Catalog. This is a closed set of annual and five-year cumulations; it lists alphabetically by subject heading the extensive holdings of the Library of Congress cataloged between 1945 and 1982. (As of 1983 it is superseded by the subject index to the microfiche *National Union Catalog;* see below). It has advantages over *Subject Guide* and the *CBI* in that it reproduces the whole catalog card for each book, enabling you to read the tracings, and it is not limited to United States or English language works. Note that this is a list of what this one library actually owns—unlike the others, it is not a list of everything that has been published. (And contrary to popular belief, the Library of Congress does not own everything that has been published. It keeps about half of the U.S. material that it receives on copyright deposit. And it acquires much more foreign-language material worldwide that any other library, although not *all* foreign books.)

When you are doing research with any of these sources, remember that they do not provide access to three additional types of sources that are especially valuable: special collections, microform collections, and government documents. (For locating special collections, see below in this chapter; for the others, see Chapter 12.) Nor do they cover journal articles, which can be identified through the various indexes, bibliographies, and databases discussed in Chapters 4 through 9.

Determining Who Owns a Copy

The two basic sources for locating copies of books are the *National Union Catalog* and the OCLC computer system. They are also useful for locating journals, but for these several special union lists of serials exist that are usually better starting points. (A union list is one that records the holdings of more than one library.)

The *National Union Catalog* has two parts, composed under separate (although similar) editorial direction: there is a huge retrospective set, and also a current, ongoing set that keeps the record up to date. It is worthwhile to consider the retrospective *National Union Catalog: Pre-1956 Imprints* in some detail.

Essentially, this *Pre-'56* set is the closest thing there is to being a list of everything published worldwide from the invention of printing through the end of 1955. That's something of an oversimplification, since no such list could ever be exhaustive. But, still, the *NUC Pre-'56* is the largest list of books ever compiled: it is a 754-volume set listing about seven to nine million items that were reported to the project by over a thousand research libraries throughout North America. It is especially valuable to researchers because, for each work listed, *it tells you which libraries actually own a copy*. Through this catalog scholars have astonishing access to the published records of the human race, in effect "direct access to the largest, richest and most open library network in the world." Among its many other uses, the *NUC* is the foundation of interlibrary loan activity. It has been called "the best record we shall ever have of the first 500 years of man's [printed] history" and "the bibliographic wonder of the world"; and indeed it is just that. Since the set is so fundamentally important to scholarship, it is worthwhile to note in detail some of its capabilities, uses, and peccadilloes—especially since these points are almost never taught in colleges and universities.

- The *National Union Catalog* is basically arranged by author (not by subject), although anonymous works are included under titles. It is thus very useful for compiling a bibliography of an author's works and their various editions. (Note, however, that it does not list individual articles within journals.)

- It lists not only books but also pamphlets, maps, atlases, broadsides, music (scores and print material rather than sound recordings), government documents, microforms, and even some manuscripts. Audiovisual materials such as phonorecords, motion pictures, and filmstrips are excluded, as are Braille and Moon books for the blind. Publications from all over the world are covered, although the emphasis is on works in the roman alphabet or Greek or Gaelic. But there are also many entries in Arabic, Cyrillic, Chinese, Japanese, Hebrew, Korean, the various Indic alphabets and other non-Latin characters. The works in the Near Eastern and Oriental alphabets are mainly those held in the vast collections of the Library of Congress.

- While the basic sources for determining library locations of journals and serials are the *Union List of Serials* and its supplement *New Serial Titles,* the *NUC* records some serials not listed in these; and it also covers conference proceedings and annual publications, which *ULS* and *NST* omit.

- The set provides very strong coverage of local, state, and federal government documents, and surprisingly good coverage of international and foreign government publications as well.

- Its overall coverage is so good that book dealers frequently raise the price of any item they come across that is not listed. "Not in *NUC*" is a strong selling point for a rare book.

- The library locations for each work are designated by symbols after the bibliographic description (Fig. 7). The most frequently used symbols are spelled out on the inside covers of each volume. Complete lists of all the symbols can be found in three volumes, 200, 560, and 754, which are bound in brown cloth so that they will stand out from the green of the others. (A common misconception regarding the *NUC* is that the Library of Congress owns every book listed in it. This is not true; LC owns only those items that have the symbol "DLC"—the D stands for District of Columbia.)

Wigram, *Sir* **James,** 1793–1866.

An examination of the rules of law, respecting the admission
-of extrinsic evidence in aid of the interpretation of wills. By
James Wigram ... 5th ed., by Charles Percy Sanger ... London, Sweet and Maxwell, limited; ¡etc., etc.¡ 1914.

xlviii, 234 p. front. (port.) 22½ᵐ.

"The text and author's notes are reprinted verbatim from the 3d ed.,
the paging of which is shown in the margin ... The 3d ed., being the last
rev. by the learned author himself, was pub. in 1840 ... The portrait of
Sir James Wigram is from a mezzotint by W. Walker, after John Watson
Gordon, ᴀ. ʀ. ᴀ."—Pref. to 5th ed.

1. Wills—Gt. Brit. 2. Evidence (Law)—Gt. Brit.   ɪ. Sanger,
Charles Percy, ed.

15—4680

NW   0293187   DLC NcD-L PPB PU-L OU CtY CaBVaU IdU MH ◄——— **Library
location symbols**

<h2 align="center">Fig. 7</h2>

Some entries do not list locations; these are in the form of "overprinted" cards. In Figure 8, for example, a work providing David
Millar Craig's biographical sketches of concert celebrities is listed
under Millar Craig's name, but no library locations are listed. In
this entry, however, "Millar Craig" is a typed-in (overprinted)
line above the main entry "Wiener, Hilda." When the main entry
card is consulted directly, library locations are found. The overprinted entries thus serve as cross-references to main entries.

• If the book you want is not in the *NUC*, you should not assume
that none of the participating libraries own it. Most of the institutions did not report every item cataloged in their collections, but
rather concentrated on those works they considered rare or unusual. Many of the participants, in fact, contributed very few reports. Several major libraries, however—the Library of Congress,
Harvard, Yale, the University of Chicago, the John Crerar, and
the New York Public—were extremely conscientious, reporting
virtually every item cataloged in their collections. Indeed, the *NUC*
lists *more* of LC's pre-1956 holdings than does LC's own public
card catalog. This is because the Library has many separate divi-
sions that have their own catalogs, and these divisional files have
large numbers of items that are not recorded in the main catalog.
The *NUC* picks up some of these divisional items.

• The *Pre-'56 NUC* consists of *two separate* A–Z alphabets: volumes 1–685 (the main sequence) and volume 686–754 (a supple-

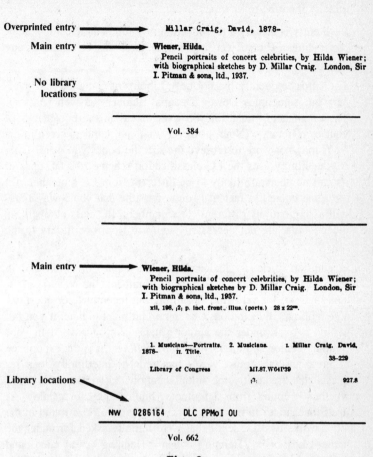

Overprinted entry ──────────► Millar Craig, David, 1878-

Main entry ──────────► Wiener, Hilda.
         Pencil portraits of concert celebrities, by Hilda Wiener;
with biographical sketches by D. Millar Craig. London, Sir
I. Pitman & sons, ltd., 1937.

No library
locations ──────────►

Vol. 384

Main entry ──────────► Wiener, Hilda.
         Pencil portraits of concert celebrities, by Hilda Wiener;
with biographical sketches by D. Millar Craig. London, Sir
I. Pitman & sons, ltd., 1937.

        xii, 198, ₍2₎ p. incl. front., illus. (ports.)   28 x 22ᶜᵐ.

        1. Musicians—Portraits. 2. Musicians.   ɪ. Millar Craig, David,
1878-   ɪɪ. Title.
                                             38-229

        Library of Congress   ML87.W64P39
                                  ₍3₎   927.8

Library locations ◄──────────

NW   0286164   DLC PPMoI OU

Vol. 662

Fig. 8

ment). The main sequence contains 11,637,350 entries and cross-references; the supplement, 949,385 (for a total of 12,586,735). It is important to note that the supplement includes many corrections and additional cross-references *to the main sequence.*

- Each of the supplementary volumes (686–754) has a separate numerically coded section that *lists additional library locations* for works already reported in the main sequence. But you should use *both* this numeric section *and* the alphabetical section of each sup-

plement volume when looking for additional locations of items
initially reported in volumes 1–685.

- Each entry is usually a reproduction of a full catalog card, including tracings. The subject headings in these can be useful in any
library.

- The cards frequently list not only Library of Congress call numbers but sometimes Dewey Decimal numbers as well (Fig. 9).
These can help you locate browsing areas in the bookstacks of
your own library . (Note, however, that call numbers given in the
NUC may not work to retrieve the specific books you want. Even
if your library uses the LC classification scheme, the tail ends of
its call numbers are likely to be different from LC's numbers for
the same books. In fact, it is quite possible that your own library
will assign entirely different class numbers. LC class numbers, in
other words, are not necessarily uniform from one library to the
next.)

- In addition to its use in locating actual copies of books and in
providing tracings and classification numbers, the *NUC* is especially helpful for verifying and filling out incomplete or questionable bibliographic citations. An important point to note: if you fail
to find a book under the author's name as you have it in your
original citation, *try slightly variant spellings*. It is the experience
of librarians who must verify hundreds of interlibrary loan requests that frequently the initial citation that readers rely on—
whether it comes from a footnote, bibliography, or catalog—is
itself inaccurate. In my own work, for example, I've found in the
NUC works by "Less*em*" that were initially asked for under the
name "Lesse*n*"; "Hennig" when "Henn*ing*" was cited; and
"Abern*e*thy" when the original footnote read "Abern*a*thy." This
approach works *with surprising frequency*.

- If an author has written a book under a pseudonym, you can often
use the *NUC* to find his or her real name. If you look under the
pen name you will find a cross-reference to the real name.

- Similarly, if an author signs initials rather than his full name, you
can use the *NUC* to find the full form. "Eliot, T.S." for example,
refers you to "Eliot, Thomas Sterns, 1888–   ." And various entries under the latter form fill in his death date at "–1965." Sim-

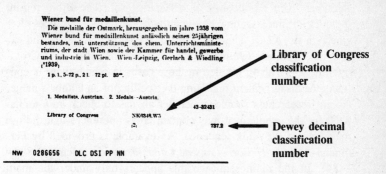

Wiener bund für medaillenkunst.

Die medaille der Ostmark, herausgegeben im jahre 1938 vom Wiener bund für medaillenkunst anlässlich seines 25jährigen bestandes, mit unterstützung des chem. Unterrichtsministeriums, der stadt Wien sowie der Kammer für handel, gewerbe und industrie in Wien. Wien-Leipzig, Gerlach & Wiedling (¹1939,

1 p. l., 5–72 p., 2 l.   72 pl.   35ᶜᵐ.

1. Medailists, Austrian.   2. Medals -Austria.

Library of Congress   NK6348.W5
                             ₍2₎

43–32431

737.2

Library of Congress classification number

Dewey decimal classification number

NW   0286656   DLC DSI PP NN

Fig. 9

ilarly, you can find that *G*ilbert *K*eith Chesterton lived from 1874–1936. Such entries and dates are useful in distinguishing among authors with similar names or initials. The first and last entry under an author's name will usually provide the fullest information.

- The *NUC* usually provides the fastest way to find out if a foreign-language book has been translated into English. If you look under the original author's name, you will find that the entries include both original-language editions and translations. (Similarly, you can often find out whether an English language book has been translated into another language.)

- Although as a rule works are entered under authors' names or under titles for anonymous works, there are many cross-references in the set that often allow you to find them under other points of access (e.g., joint author, compiler, translator of poetry or drama, honoree of *Festschriften,* name of artist in cases of works with art reproductions). *Editors'* names, however, are usually *not* used as access points. The main entry point for most U.S. government documents (vols. 609–624) begins with the corporate designation "United States," subdivided by department, bureau, or office—but since this makes items difficult to find, the editors also included rather liberal cross-references under titles or authors' personal names for these works. Similarly, the works in the "Bible" volumes (53–56) appear rather liberally under other entry points as well. (It is noteworthy that the U.S. documents volumes and

the Bible listings are such large catalogs in their own right that
each has been republished as a separate set. The Bible reprint
includes an index volume that cumulates the cross-references elsewhere in the *NUC*. There are also one-volume reprints of the extensive ''Catholic Church'' and ''Freemasons'' listings.) Cross-
references are also provided in those cases in which there is confusion or disagreement regarding the spelling of an author's name.
Again, researchers should remember always to check *both* alphabets, for the supplement may contain cross-references that did not
make it into the main sequence. An example is provided by Ferdinand Andre's *Deliberations de l'administration* (Mende, 1882–
1884). In the main sequence this appears only under the main
entry ''Lozere, France (dept.).'' However, if you look in the supplement under ''Andre, Ferdinand'' you will find a cross-reference that refers you to the ''Lozere'' entry.

- Regrettably, many books held by Pennsylvania libraries and recorded in the Union Library Catalog of Pennsylvania are not listed
in the *NUC*, due to disagreements among those involved. If you
don't find an item you want in the *NUC*, and wish to double-
check Pennsylvania holdings—an especially wise course of action
if you need to locate a work published in that state—send a stamped,
self-addressed envelope with your request to the Union Library
Catalog, 3401 Market St., Philadelphia, Pa. 19104 (215 382-5104).
(Note, however, that many Pennsylvania libraries reporting their
holdings to the Pennsylvania catalog *also* reported directly to the
NUC.)

- All works listed in the *Pre-'56 NUC* were published, obviously,
prior to 1956. However, the cut-off date for libraries to report
such books was in late 1977; and about 639,000 pre-'56 publications and additional locations reported after that date did not make
it into the *Pre-'56 NUC*, nor have they been included in any of
the supplements after 1956 (i.e., the ongoing *NUC*). The cards
for this extra file still exist in a Library of Congress warehouse;
however, they have not been edited or arranged in any searchable
order. As of this writing no decision has been made to publish
them.

- Researchers should be aware of seven other national union catalogs maintained in card-file format at the Library of Congress,

which the regular *NUC* overlaps but does not supersede. These are for foreign-language materials in non-roman scripts; they are:

Japanese Union Catalog (ca. 700,000 cards)
Chinese Union Catalog (ca. 900,000 cards)
Korean Union Catalog (ca. 110,000 cards)
Hebraic/Yiddish Union Catalog (ca. 500,000 cards)
Ladino Union Catalog (ca. 9,000 cards)
Near East Union Catalog (Arabic, Persian, and Turkish; ca. 160,000 cards)
Slavic/Cyrillic Union Catalog (ca. 500,000 cards).

These files contain entries, with library locations, for materials in non-Roman scripts *originally cataloged by libraries other than LC.* They also contain items originally cataloged by LC and which therefore appear in the regular *NUC;* but the other non-LC entries—and there are literally millions of them—are not in the *NUC.* All these card files are kept up to date, some of them with separate "Add-on" sections that cover reports received from 1981 and afterwards, which may be cataloged under different rules. The *Near East Union List* is also available in database form; and the *Slavic/Cyrillic Catalog* is also commercially available in microfiche. The Library also maintains two other separate national union catalogs, one of talking books and books in Braille for blind and physically handicapped people; this exists in database form. The other, the National Union Index to Architectural Records, consists of reports of collections of architectural records throughout the country; currently it has about 1500 cards.

• If you want to impress a librarian with a bit of trivia, mention that you've found a circular entry in the *Pre-'56.* When you look up Kaspar Hedio's *Chronica der Alten Christlichen Kirchen* (vol. 238, p. 43, col. 3) you'll find a note to "See under Eusebius Pamphilii, bp. of Caesarea." But when you look this up (vol. 163, p. 442, col. 3) you'll find a "see" reference directing you back to "Hedio, Kaspar." (And then mention that your further research has discovered that the mistake is corrected in the supplement, vol. 773, p. 270, col. 2.)

• If you want to be truly obnoxious in your expertise, mention that you strongly disagree with the note written by a disgruntled *NUC* employee and inserted on the card for James Wolveridge's *Speculum Matricis* (vol. 671); and that you have grave doubts about the bibliographic veracity of entry #NP0576549 (vol. 471), which you have determined is *not* owned by the University of Oregon.

- The physical size of the *Pre-'56* set is staggering. Most of its 754 volumes weigh about 7½ pounds each, for a total of almost three tons. A complete set has about 528,000 pages, taking up 125 linear feet of shelving. It has been estimated that, thrown from volume 1 toward the end of the set, the world's record shot-put would reach only to volume 453; and that, had the Wright brothers' first airplane flight started at volume 1, it would have ended five feet short of the end of the set. Also, if all the 14″ high volumes of one set were balanced on top of each other, the column would be over 1½ times the height of the Washington Monument.

- The entire *Pre-'56 NUC* is also now available in a microfiche set.

- One of the interesting by-products of the compilation of the set was the discovery that some widely held assumptions about research libraries are false. Gordon R. Williams, Chairman of the National Union Catalog subcommittee within the American Library Association, has pointed out the surprising finding:

In 1901 when Librarian of Congress Herbert Putnam started the union catalog, the implicit assumption was that—except where libraries had pursued special interests—the main differences between collections were determined by the age and size of the individual libraries in which they were housed. It was assumed that all comparable research libraries held in common virtually the same core collection and that it was essentially the older and larger libraries that were the repositories of books not generally to be found in the younger and smaller ones. This belief is implicit in Putnam's view, expressed in his annual report for 1900, that with the completion of the filing of cards from Harvard, the Boston Public Library, the New York Public Library, and a few others, the union catalog would "constitute the closest approximation now available to a complete record of books in American libraries."

The following facts, which many librarians still find difficult to believe, did not become clear until much later. Research library collections, even those of about the same age, size, and purpose, hold many fewer titles in common than everyone thought. Far more titles and editions are held by only one or very few of them. And, anything even approaching a complete record of books in American libraries requires a union catalog of hundreds of libraries.[1]

Scholars in America are therefore especially fortunate to have a resource such as the *NUC* at their disposal—no other nation has anything like it. (The largest catalogs of other countries, e.g., those for the British Library or the Bibliotheque Nationale, are not union lists; they are catalogs of only the holdings of the one national library.)

The ongoing *National Union Catalog*—as distinct from the *Pre-'56 NUC*—consists of five-year cumulations and annual bound volumes for the years after the *Pre-'56* up through the end of 1982; from 1983 onwards it is published only in microfiche format. The hard-copy volumes through 1982 contain reports only of material published in 1956 or afterwards; they do not provided additional reports or locations of pre-1956 imprints. Starting with the fiche in 1983, however, imprints and locations of *all* dates are recorded. Also, as of 1983 there is now access by four separate indexes: author, title, LC subject headings, and series.

With the post-1955 *NUC* reports of location of items—i.e., which libraries own a copy—are not always provided on the bibliographic entries themselves but rather are sometimes given in a supplemental list called the *Register of Additional Locations*. As of the conversion of the publication to microfiche in 1983, locations are primarily reported in the separate fiche register of locations, and not with the bibliographic entries themselves; the only "location" with the record itself will be the symbol of the library that created the record, not the list of all the libraries that own copies. The complete *RAL* exists in two five-year bound sets, 1963–1967 and 1968–1972, plus cumulative microfiche sets issued quarterly thereafter (each cumulation entirely replaces the previous microfiche set).

The *NUC* is in a sense another competitor of the OCLC computer system; however, each contains information that is not in the other. (For a fuller discussion of OCLC searches, see Chapter 9.) OCLC usually provides more locations for each reported item and is updated faster. The *NUC*, on the other hand, covers many libraries not on the OCLC system; indeed, to some extent it spans libraries in all the OCLC, RLIN, WLN, and UTLAS systems. And the fiche product is likely to be found in many more libraries than have direct access to a computer network.

There is a somewhat similar union list of *Music* publications put out by the Library of Congress, except that it includes reports from only about eight libraries. LC's *Audiovisual* materials list, formerly hard copy and now on microfiche, includes only LC's own holdings. *The National Union Catalog of Manuscript Collections* (also published by LC), however, reports holdings from libraries all over the country. Each of these three has a subject index that uses the vocabulary of *LC Subject Headings*. An additional microfiche set, *NUC Cartographic Materials*, has an index by a Geographic Classification Code.

For locating copies of journals several good sources are usually better than the *NUC* and OCLC, especially if the journal is an older one. The basic sets are the *Union List of Serials (ULS)* and its supplements, called *New Serial Titles (NST)*. These are arranged by titles of journals, and for each they tell which libraries in North America own sets. Mercifully, they are hard-copy publications, not microfiche.

A number of specialized union lists cover journal holdings in particular regions (e.g., *California Union List of Periodicals, Journal Holdings in the Washington-Baltimore Area*); or on particular subjects (e.g., *Union List of Military Periodicals, Union List of Population Family Planning Periodicals*); or in particular formats (e.g., *Union List of Little Magazines, Union List of Newspapers*). There are also union lists of serials for some other countries (e.g., *British Union-Catalogue of Periodicals, Catalog Collectif des Periodiques*). And then there are combinations of subject and area holdings (e.g., *Union List of Statistical Serials in British Libraries; Art Serials: Union List of Art Periodicals and Serials in Research Libraries in the Washington DC Metropolitan Area*). *Hundreds* of such specialized lists exist; they can be identified with the help of reference librarians.

Determining Which Libraries Have Special Collections on Your Subject

No matter how good the coverage of the *NUC* and OCLC and the various other union lists and databases, libraries will always have many items that are recorded only on their own premises. And so you may wish to determine which facilities simply have good collections or

special holdings in your area of interest, for browsing or further research. There are two good sources for determining the existence and
location of subject collections throughout the country, and a third for
libraries in other countries. The overall sources are:

1. *Subject Collections,* compiled by Lee Ash (New York: Bowker,
   revised irregularly). This is the basic guide to well over 10,000
   special collections in university, college, public, and special libraries and museums in the United States and Canada. Entries are arranged alphabetically according to *Library of Congress Subject
   Headings* (with additional subject terms as needed); each provides
   the address of the library, an estimate of the number of items in
   the collection, and, frequently, descriptive notes.

2. *Directory of Special Libraries and Information Centers,* edited by
   Louis Lenroot-Ernt (Detroit: Gale Research, revised irregularly).
   This lists and describes 16,000 facilities in the United States and
   Canada, and has a detailed subject index. A particularly useful fea-
   ture is its geographic index, which will tell you quickly which li-
   braries are in your area.

3. *World Guide to Special Libraries,* edited by Helga Legenfelder
   (Munich: K.G. Saur, 1983; distributed by Gale). This lists 32,000
   libraries in 159 countries. It is divided into five major categories
   (general, humanities, social sciences, medical/health sciences, science and technology) and has a 212-page subject index.

As with union lists, there are also many specialized guides to libraries in particular regions within this country and to those in other
countries (e.g., *Special Collections in German Libraries; Subject Collections in European Libraries*); the librarians in your area can tell you
which ones exist locally; the sources in Chapter 13 can be used to
identify the others.

The United States is particularly blessed with an excellent interlibrary loan (ILL) network. If you cannot find the book or article you
want within your area, be sure to ask your librarians about the possibilities of borrowing the item from another facility, or of acquiring a
photocopy. It is best to first ask through a library; if this doesn't work,
or if the item cannot be borrowed or photocopied through interlibrary
loan, then contact the holding institution directly. Sometimes it will
have photocopy or microfilming procedures outside the ILL network;

or it can give you the names of local researchers for hire who can make photocopies for you.

The overall point to keep in mind is that if you have identified a good source that is not available in your local library, don't give up. The same local library is likely to have the means of identifying which other libraries either have the desired item or are likely to have it.

Note

1. Gordon R. Williams, *"The National Union Catalog* and Research Libraries," in *In Celebration: The National Union Catalog, Pre-1956 Imprints,* edited by John Y. Cole (Washington, D.C.: Library of Congress, 1981), p. 14.

11

Talking to People

So far we have examined six major avenues of access to information: controlled vocabulary searches, systematic browsing, key word searches, citation searches, searches through published bibliographies, and those done through computers. (Computer searches use elements of the other methods but add the possibility of post-coordinate Boolean combinations.) The seventh major avenue—that of talking to people—is the one most favored by journalists, but it is also valuable for anyone else.

It is particularly important for academic researchers to be aware of this method, as most academics have an overly strong print bias, that is, they often unconsciously assume that if information cannot be found in print, then it cannot be found at all. This mental set is frequently complicated by two other assumptions, that calling people on the phone is "bothering" them, and that spending a few dollars on long-distance calls is totally beyond the pale of acceptable behavior.

Such attitudes can be very detrimental to quality research, particularly if the timeliness of information is important. Even the most recent journal articles may be several months old due to the time-lag involved in submission, acceptance, and publication of manuscripts. Regardless of the time factor, however, talking to people will be valuable in any event because an expert can usually provide you with information that has never existed in printed form.

It may seem obvious to state this; and, indeed, I have found few people who would say that they disagree with these observations. Still—

and this is the problem—many people who intellectually know that doing good research must take them outside the four walls of a library will not *act* as though they know it. When it finally comes to *doing* research, they are quite reluctant to go beyond print sources to find what they want.

Part of the difficulty lies in the way "Research methods" courses are taught in colleges. Very often they are confined to the discussion of a relatively few sources on a prescribed bibliography, and correlative assignments are frequently made with the stipulation that "you have to use the sources on this list" coupled with "don't bother the reference librarians—you should do your research on your own." Unfortunately, students tend unwittingly to learn more than they should from such experiences: they learn that "doing research" equals "playing library games" and that talking to people is "bothering" them and may even have a faint scent of "cheating" to it. Professors seem unaware of the long-term damage this does, not only to their students' subsequent academic careers but also to the future satisfaction of their curiosity about topics of personal interest. Reference librarians, on the other hand, notice the limiting effects of such "learning" all the time.

Genuine learning should obviously be a broadening rather than a limiting experience; and in doing research the most important lesson to learn is that *any* source is fair game. One should always go to wherever the information needed is most likely to be, and very often this will be in someone's head rather than in a book. (Remember, too, though, that you can travel "full circle" from talking to an expert to get back into the literature—for usually the expert will know the *best* written sources, and can thereby offer valuable shortcuts that will make library research much more efficient.)

Talking to people can provide insights into one's own area of research, feedback on problem points, and a structure of perception that written sources often cannot match. Also, conversations are particularly important for revealing which areas of inquiry are valuable and worth pursuing, and which are likely to waste time.

Still, a word of caution is in order: a judicious mixture of conversations and print sources is often the ideal in doing good research. Just as academics tend to overemphasize print, so journalists tend to emphasize interviews to the outright neglect of print sources. Each can learn from the other.

Contrary to widespread assumption, it does not take special training or credentials to do research by telephone or interview. Indeed, there is a notable research company in Washington that has charged its clients over $75 per hour to find information on anything from the market for golf carts in the United States, to eggplants, to abrasives, to the marketability of rubber-soled shoes in Eastern Europe—and without its researchers having any more background in these areas *than you do right now*. The president of the company has said:

> The information [which clients want] is usually somewhere in the federal government. The problem most people have is that they don't know how to find it. They make 10 calls, get transferred around and still don't get the right person. So they get frustrated and give up. . . .
>
> We have a former French pastry chef and an ex-seminarian. We look for people who make others want to talk to them and aren't intimidated by getting into a new topic every day.
>
> Sometimes you're better off if you're not a hotshot specialist. Then it's easy to know how hard it might be to find something. Ignorance is bliss in a lot of research projects.[1]

The fact that people without "credentials' can charge $75 per hour for making telephone calls points up two very important things: the technique of talking to people *does* produce good results, no matter what the subject; and *anyone can do it*.

The key factors for success are not experience and credentials but rather your attitudes and assumptions. All you have to do is to start somewhere, and then follow through in asking questions. In other words, just jump in and do it. The main stumbling block most researchers have is their own inhibiting belief that people will not respond. But most interviewees are flattered that you would consider them knowledgeable in some area, and they will almost always respond helpfully. Experience will show you that the odds are in your favor—telephone or other contacts will usually be friendly, and people will sometimes volunteer much more information than you originally request.

If you start with *any* negative assumption, you will be defeating yourself before you even begin. If the reasons for not making a phone call seem stronger than the reasons to go ahead and do it, then you're dooming yourself to failure. Most of these "reasons" will be only rationalizations to justify your own unwarranted shyness. Your attitude should be, simply, "What have I got to lose?" The answer is "Nothing"—or at worst, a few dollars for a long distance call; and frequently people will spend much more than that on amusements much less important to their happiness than good information.

The results are likely to repay you amply in time saved on complicated library searches. For example, one researcher trying to find "Who syndicates Interlandi?" simply called the National Press Club and found the information. Another person looking for the address of a company in Japan couldn't find it in any of the library directories, so he just called the Japanese embassy and got the information from a staff member. Another student seeking information on the little-known winner of the Nobel Peace Prize, Adolfo Perez Esquivel, could find nothing on him in library resources at the time he won the prize; but calls to Amnesty International and the Washington Office on Latin America provided a whole file of information.

Talking to people can provide you with a quick overview of a whole field; it can give you not only the anwer to a question but the larger context in which the question should be asked. For example, someone who was looking for information on the U.S. market for padlocks imported from India first did considerable library research; but only in talking to knowledgeable people in the field did he really get oriented. He was told that there are six different grades of padlocks, which have different markets; that it's best to concentrate on small areas as data on large areas is unreliable; that there were forthcoming national standards for padlocks, which imported items might have to meet in another year or two; that he should first have the locks tested for quality (using current military specifications as interim standards, if applicable to the grade of item being imported) and have a written contract that all other locks will be comparable, before paying for any; that he should incorporate in order to prevent personal bankruptcy in case a class action suit should result from the sale of a defective lock; that he must consider not only the price of the items but also the import duty and shipping charges; and that the big chain stores will certainly be able to buy more cheaply than he, so his best bet is to market through independent "Mom and Pop" type hardware stores.

The experts that this researcher talked to not only provided him with answers, they also alerted him to *whole new areas of questions* that he had to consider, none of which he had thought of on his own. It's often impossible to get this kind of corrective feedback from printed sources, as they allow no interaction with the reader, nor can they be modified on the spot to accommodate slightly different inquiries. For this kind of thing you just have to talk to someone. (Note that even letter writing is a poor substitute for a telephone call, although it's a good complement or means of follow-up.)

Some recalcitrant souls will undoubtedly still be intimidated by their lack of "credentials," even though lack of training is irrelevant to their success. For academics, it is to be hoped that the obvious will allay their fears: they already have research credentials precisely because of their university affiliation. The best way to start off a telephone conversation with a potential source is to mention this right up front: "I'm a student/grad student at _____ University, and I'm not sure whom I should talk to—maybe you could help, or direct me to the right person. I'm trying to find information on . . ."

Those who don't have any affiliation can do just as well.[2] In obtaining information, the "secret" that is so hard for so many people to believe is this: *There is no secret. Just make the call anyway and be perfectly honest about your reasons. It's O.K. to ask for help. The odds are that you'll succeed if you are simply persistent in developing a chain of referrals.*

Only a few things must be kept in mind to make your calls productive. First, if the nature of your inquiry is particularly complex, do a little homework first. At least talk to the reference librarians of your local library to see if they can suggest some background reading for orientation. An expert will be more helpful if you convey the impression that you've already done some work on your own and are willing to do more—and that you're not simply dumping the whole problem in his or her lap to solve for you.

Second, explain the purpose of your research—that is, what you're *ultimately* trying to do, and what you will use the information for (e.g., personal curiosity, publication, broadcast, etc.). Be open and honest about it; and try to be as specific as you can. If you ask specific questions, you're likely to get on-target answers; but if you ask only vague, general questions, you're likely to get only vague, general answers.

Third, respect the expert's intellectual property rights. Don't simply "milk" a person for information and then pass it off as your own—be careful not to infringe on your source's own potential use of the information. People who burn their sources in this way not only ruin their own chances for follow-up contacts, they may also make the source hesitant about helping any other researchers. Anyone who uses "the network" has a responsibility to leave it in good or better shape for the next person.

Fourth, when you talk to people about a subject you're not familiar with, it is very important to ask for more contacts. Few researchers will rely exclusively on one printed source; it is similarly unwise to rely on only one spoken viewpoint. People's memories of events, and opinions, tend to be self-serving; it is therefore advisable to seek a balance of perspectives. (A related problem in some inquiries is that of "shrinkage of testimony." Private investigators and journalists frequently run into this. Sometimes a source will be very garrulous and free with statements when you first talk to him; but if he is later subject to cross-examination by an unsympathetic interrogator, or if he comes to realize that he will somehow be held accountable for his opinions, he may have much less to say. This points up one advantage of a printed source: it will be the same no matter how often you refer to it. There is also, of course, a corresponding disadvantage: the situation may have changed dramatically since the words were printed.)

And fifth, after you have talked to someone who has been helpful—especialy if the person has gone out of his or her way for you—it is very important to write a thank you note. There are several reasons for this:

- Above all, if a person has helped you it is simply appropriate to show your gratitude.

- A written record of your interest in a subect will enable your source to remember you, and to use *you* as a possible future source of information on your shared area of interest. This is how mutually beneficial contact networks are built up.

- You will frequently find that, days later when you are finally writing your report, new questions will occur to you which you did not think to ask the first time. When you call your source again for clarification, he will be more responsive if he's already received a good thank you in writing, for such notes are useful to him in very concrete ways. They provide proofs of good job performance that he can readily refer to for justifying raises, program extensions, and so on.

- The *lack* of a thank you note can positively hurt you when you want to use a source again. This writer is aware of more than one

instance in which contacts who had no obligation to help researchers nevertheless went out of their way to provide information—
and never received any thanks for their efforts. The result was
that, in each case, the contacts "dried up" when the same people
sought them again for more information.

When you are paying someone to help you, you can call that
person at any time. But when you are getting information for free,
you must at all costs avoid the appearance of being thankless or
pushy. It is therefore advisable to consider the sending of timely
thank you notes not simply as a nice thing to do, but rather as *an
integral part of the research process.* If you haven't put a word
of thanks *in writing,* you have not finished the contact with your
source.

The problem remains, then, that even if you do want to talk to
someone who knows about your subject, how do you find that person?
Where do you start? If your own circle of acquaintances doesn't get
you far enough, many sources will be useful, among them the following:

Washington Information Directory (Congressional Quarterly, annual). This is a subject guide to agencies of the executive branch, to
Congress and its committees and subcommittees, and to private and
nongovernmental organizations. It describes each organization, gives
a summary of its area of interest, and provides specific phone numbers
and addresses. Chapters include sources in sixteen broad categories:

Communication and the media
Congress and politics
Economics and business
Education and culture
Employment and labor
Energy
Equal rights (minorities, women)
Government personnel and services
Health and consumer affairs
Housing and urban affairs
Individual assistance programs
International affairs
Law and justice

National security
Natural resources, environment, and agriculture
Science, space and transportation

Each chapter has further subdivisions, and there is a detailed index to the whole volume.

The value of having this information network at your call (and it *is* available to anyone) is incalculable. The federal government is an especially good place to begin looking for subject experts, as it employs thousands in mid-level positions in the bureaucracy. These people spend their careers keeping abreast of information in limited areas, and all of these subject specialists can be reached by phone. (Note that you should first seek the specialists themselves in the department or agency—not the librarians in the agency's library.) They are quite helpful—and, in fact, *you* are helpful to *them,* since in answering inquiries from the public they justify their jobs, programs, and salaries. They can also refer you to excellent private and nongovernmental contacts. The researcher mentioned above who was working on padlocks started out with the *Washington Information Directory* and then just followed a chain of referrals from the Commerce Department to various private sources.

Researchers Guide to Washington Experts.   This directory, from Washington Researchers, is a subject-indexed guide to 15,000 experts within the federal government, including 800 in the Department of Agriculture, 1500 in Commerce, 500 in Energy, 300 in the Labor Department, and 700 at Treasury. It gives specific names and phone numbers.

Carroll Publishing Company directories.   There are a number of these: *Federal Executive Directory, Federal Regional Executive Directory, State Executive Directory, Municipal Executive Directory,* and *County Executive Directory.* Again, the advantage of government sources is that agencies employ experts in a wide range of subject areas, and all of them can be contacted for free. Further, state and local people may well have better information on some subjects than federal sources have.

Encyclopedia of Associations.   Associations and professional societies are excellent switchboards for connecting researchers with highly qualified sources. Indeed, the very purpose of most societies is to study and disseminate information or points of view on particular subjects, so they will welcome inquiries that enable them to tell you more about themselves and their areas of interest. The annual *Encyclopedia,* from Gale Research, is the best list there is of such groups; it describes over 20,000 nonprofit American membership organizations of national scope, and a separate volume covers thousands of foreign associations. Each entry provides the address, telephone number, and name of the organization's chief official, plus a detailed description of the society's area of interest and purpose. There is also information on the society's publications, and dates and city locations of upcoming conventions. The volume has a comprehensive index by organizations' names and by key words.

There is a society for everything under the sun. The following brief list gives only the slightest hint of the range and diversity of such groups:

American Society of Abdominal Surgery
Abortion (over 200 societies, pro and con)
International Chinese Snuff Bottle Society
Carbonated Beverage Institute
Dance (over 50 organizations)
Estonian Educational Society
National Association of Franchise Companies
Gemnological Institute of America
Baker Street Irregulars (Sherlock Holmes buffs)
Society for Siberian Irises
John Milton Society
American Kiteflying Association
Federation of Historical Bottle Clubs
Life Insurance (over two dozen groups)
Mansucript Society
National Conference of Tuberculosis Secretaries
National Outdoor Drama Association
Frozen Onion Ring Packers Council
National Quartz Producers Council
National Ice Cream Retailers Association
Survival and Flight Equipment Association
American Schizophrenic Association

Tapes for the Blind
American Institute for Ultrasonics in Medicine
Veterinarians (over 60 societies)
Western Retail Lumberman's Assocation
Stunt Women of America
International Organization of Women Executives
American Society of X-Ray Technicians
Young Socialist Alliance
Zugzwang! Postal Chess Association

The *Encyclopedia of Associations* is a publication that everyone should browse through; it's useful not only for research but also for finding people who have the same hobby as you.

Yellow Pages.　This incredible subject directory of the resources of your own area is one of the best possible starting points for handling many questions, yet it is often overlooked by those who think research can be done only in libraries. Added features are a ZIP Code map of the area and a detailed index, which is the necessary key to the controlled vocabulary subject headings used in the book. (Remember, too, that your local library may have a set of Yellow Pages for other cities throughout the country.)

Directory of Directories (Detroit: Information Enterprises, annual; distributed by Gale Research); supplemented by inter-edition *Directory Information Service.*　The *Directory* describes approximately 10,000 sources in sixteen broad subject categories; there are also detailed Subject and Title indexes. Price and ordering information are included for each listing. Just as there is an organization for everything under the sun, so, too, there is a directory of contacts on any subject. The following is a sampling of the directories available:

Adventure Travel
Directory of Adult Day Care Centers
Directory of Medical Specialists
Fine Arts Marketplace
Earthworm Buyer's Guide
Directory of Conventions
Minority Organizations: A National Directory
Directory of American Occult and Paranormal

Crime and Detective Fiction: A Handbook of Dealers and Collectors in Britain and Wales

Opportunities for Study in Hand Bookbinding and Calligraphy

International Directory of Published Market Research

National Directory for the Performing Arts/Educational [Schools and programs]

Directory of Genealogical Societies in the U.S.A. and Canada

List of Shopowners

Mail Order Business Directory

Directory of Golf Course Architects

Maryland State Industrial Directory

List of Cryo-Surgeons [Hemorrhoid specialists]

Information Market Place

Auto Enthusiasts Directory

Seasonal Employment [National Park Service]

Shopper's Guide to Museum Stores

National Register of Certified Sex Educators, Certified Sex Therapists

Toll Free Digest: A Directory of Toll Free Telephone Numbers

Exotic Weapons

The *Directory of Directories* also lists local directories for specific areas, under the names of cities in the Subject Index.

Writer's Resource Guide, edited by Bernardine Clark (Cincinnati: Writer's Digest Books, 1983). This is an excellent directory of sources (with phone numbers) for authors who need facts in any subject field.

Faculty of local universities. The professors at institutions of higher learning are experts on an astonishing variety of topics, and most maintain regular office hours in which they are available for consultation or simply "chewing the fat." An advantage to researchers here is that there is no problem in getting past secretaries during these office hours—the scholars are there for the purpose of being available to all comers.

Authors of books or articles that you've already read. Writers who have published something on a particular subject usually keep up to date on new developments in the field. Such people can be located through various directories available in libraries and through publishers' offices.

These sources should be more than adequate for leading you to knowledgeable people in any field. Two additional sources with useful "how to" tips are John Brady's *The Craft of Interviewing* (New York: Vintage Books, 1976) and Senator William S. Cohen and Kenneth Larson's *Getting the Most Out of Washington* (New York: Facts on File, 1982). The latter describes, through many detailed case studies, what a member of Congress's office can do to pull strings for you.

A further word of advice has to do specifically with talking to reference librarians. Just as it is useful to match your book-retrieval techniques to the library's storage techniques, so it is often advisable to match the way you ask questions to the way librarians think (and any group that can hide books on "Adolescent suicide" under "Youth—Suicidal behavior" obviously doesn't think like most people).

Actually, it is the librarian's professional responsibility to find out what you're ultimately looking for—which may not be what you request initially—through a reference interview; so if you wind up being directed to an inappropriate source it may be more the librarian's fault than your own. Still, even if the misdirection isn't your error, you will nevertheless want to avoid it; and if you can make the librarian's job a little easier by knowing the sort of information he or she is listening for, then you will be the one to benefit. Going with the grain is more efficient that going against it.

Three examples of what to be aware of:

- A woman asked a librarian, "Where are your books on nineteenth-century English history?" The reference interview, however, elicited the fact that what she really wanted was, specifically, biographical information about her ancestor Samuel Earnshaw. Once this had been determined, the librarian referred her directly to the multivolume set *Modern English Biography,* which contained the necessary information. (*Biography and Genealogy Master Index* also provided other sources.) Had the librarian simply referred her to the library's bookstacks on nineteenth-century English history, the woman would have wasted much time.

- Another woman asked a graduate library assistant "Where is *Chemical Abstracts?*" Further questioning could not elicit her ultimate aim, and so she was indeed referred to *CA.* After about an hour, however, she came back and the assistant asked if she'd found what she needed. She had not. "What I'm really trying to find," she added, "is information on the side effects of Valium." Once the graduate student knew this, she could refer her directly to the *Physician's Desk Reference* manual, which the woman had never heard of.

- A student asked a reference librarian "Where are your books on English literature?" After some discussion the librarian finally determined that he specifically wanted critical articles on Sir Walter Scott's *The Heart of Midlothian*. The student could then be referred to *English Novel Explication: Criticism to 1972* (among other sources), which lists such criticisms. Had the librarian simply referred him to the PR (English literature) section of the classification scheme, the student would have wasted a lot of time in the stacks and still not found what he needed. (Journal articles are very difficult to find through browsing.)

In each of these cases—and librarians could cite thousands more—the inquirers asked *not for what they really wanted but for what they thought the library could provide.* The problem is that most people have grossly inadequate assumptions about what can or cannot be found in a library. Others tend to think that the few resources or indexes they've heard about are the only or the best ones that exist. *They are usually wrong.*

Frequently, professors and graduate students are more inefficient than anyone else. This hearkens back to a point made earlier, that a large number of them have never critically challenged the dictum passed on to generation after generation of graduate students all over the country: "You shouldn't have to ask a librarian for help; if you can't find it on your own, you're no scholar." Researchers who have more common sense will not thus cut themselves off from a major source of help. The "find it on your own" imperative not only prevents scholars from asking for help, it also encourages them to settle for whatever they do find on their own, even when it's not exactly what they want. Even worse, when scholars can't think of a likely source offhand, this mentality encourages them to give up searching in the first place and to pretend that they don't really need what they think they can't get. Or just as bad—and this is a relatively new development—it encourages them to put inordinate trust in computer searches, which they wrongly assume will cover "everything."

That dictum is bad advice. Phrased positively, however—and

understood positively—it is good advice: "The more you understand of library sources and systems, the better the scholar you will be." To the extent that you learn the range and depth of what you can expect from a library, you will allow yourself to ask more questions—and especially specific questions—which you might otherwise think could not be answered efficiently. You will then find yourself asking "Where can I find biographical information on my ancestor Samuel Earnshaw, who lived in nineteenth-century England?" rather than "Where are your books on nineteenth-century English history?" You will ask, "Where can I find information on the side effects of Valium?" rather than "Where is *Chemical Abstracts?*" You will inquire, "Where can I find criticisms of Scott's *Heart of Midlothian?*" rather than "Where are your books on English literature?"

What is most useful to a reference librarian is to know what you are *ultimately* trying to find. A good way to clarify your thoughts on this is to ask yourself, "If there were an absolutely perfect article on my subject, what would the title of that article be?"

In going *outside* the library to talk to people, however, you will need some good directories, and therefore your library should have an up-to-date shelf of them. (A good rule of thumb is that 30% of the entries in any directory of personal names changes from one year to the next, so a directory more than two years old is not very trustworthy. A directory of institutions, however, may be good for much longer.)

The rule to remember on all of this is that somewhere along the line in your research you should ask yourself, "Who would be likely to know about this subject? Whose *business* is it to know? Whose *interest* would it be?" These questions, plus a browsing familiarity with the directories listed above, can get you started on some very valuable pathways, and lead you to important information that is not recorded in any print source.

Notes

1. Leila Kight, quoted in the *Washington Post*, April 15, 1980, p. B5.

2. Unaffiliated scholars will find Ronald Gross's *The Independent Scholar's Handbook* (Reading, Mass.: Addison-Wesley, 1982) very useful.

12

Hidden Treasures

Three types of library holdings contain an incredible wealth of information in all subject areas, but are so neglected by most conventional catalogs and indexes that they are virtually unknown to most researchers. Discovering any one of them, however, can provide you with the reader's equivalent of tapping into Alaska's north shore oil reserves. The three are microform sets, government documents, and special collections. These materials have several points in common:

- In addition to being neglected by most card catalogs, indexes, and databases, they are usually housed in quarters that are physically separate from a library's general collections.

- They are not shelved in a way that allows efficient subject access through browsing.

- They are each accessible only through a variety of special indexes, not through a single convenient source; and the identification of the best indexes may be a separate treasure hunt in itself.

It takes extra steps to get into these materials, in other words, and few people bother because to those lacking prior experience in these areas the paths are very obscure and the destination isn't foreseeable. Those who have enough faith to venture off the beaten track, however, are usually well rewarded. But you simply have to suspect in advance that microform sets, government documents, and special collections will indeed yield remarkable results, and then actively look for them—for you cannot expect the normal channels of research to turn up adequate references to them. And in seeking these materials it is especially important to ask for help, for frequently the best initial access is through the experienced custodian's knowledge of what is likely to be found in the collections.

The ways to identify special collections have been discussed above in Chapter 10 and so will not be repeated here.

Microform Sets

Many researchers are initially deterred from using microforms by the mistaken assumption that they cannot make quick photocopies on paper from such formats. But the truth is that such copies can be made very easily, and that any library with microfilm or microfiche holdings will also have a reader-printer immediately adjacent to them. Photocopies usually cost about 20¢ per page. Researchers who need copies made from opaque formats (i.e., microcards or microprint), however, do have a problem. Even the Library of Congress does not have a machine that can make hard copy from these. But if you are faced with this difficulty, you can still solve it by writing to one of the publishers of these formats, which will supply photostatic copies at the rate of about 30¢ per page (price subject to change). Their address is: Readex Microprint Corporation, c/o Boston Public Library, Copley Square, Boston, Mass. 02216 (617 536-5828). Reproductions are also available from the company's main office: Readex Microprint Corporation, 58 Pine Street, New Canaan, Conn. 06840 (203 966-5906).

There are hundreds of large, prepackaged research collections in a bewildering variety of subject areas, and there is likely to be one or more of interest to any scholar. The best starting point is Suzanne Dodson's *Microform Research Collections: A Guide* (Meckler Publishing, 1984). It will tell you which ones exist and describe them in detail; it also has a good subject index. Also useful is the annual *Subject Guide to Microforms in Print,* which lists collections, individual publications, and serials but does not describe or annotate them.

Once you have determined from Dodson which collections you would like to see, the problem remains as to which libraries own those collections. The best way to check in your local area is through a few phone calls; or in some areas there may be a local union list of microform holdings. Nationally, your best bet is to contact the Association of Research Libraries Microform Project (202 232-2466) at 1527 New Hampshire Ave. N.W., Washington, D.C. 20036, which has information on the holdings of over five hundred U.S. and Canadian libraries and also on various finding aids available in particular geographical areas.

The range and variety of the sets that exist can be suggested by a brief listing of some of their titles.

African Library
American Architectural Books
American Natural History
American Fiction, 1774–1900; 1901–1910
American Poetry, 1609–1900
Botany Library on Microfiche
British and Continental Rhetoric and Elocution
British Periodicals in the Creative Arts
City Directories of the United States [1786–1901]
Crime and Juvenile Delinquency
Documents on Contemporary China 1949–1975
Early American Imprints, 1639–1800; 1801–1819
Early English Books, 1475–1640; 1641–1700
Eighteenth Century Collection
French Revolution: Critical Works and Historical Sources
Goldsmiths'-Kress Library of Economic Literature
Herstory
History of Medicine
History of Women
Human Relations Area Files
Human Rights Documents
Indians of North America
Kentucky Culture
Landmarks of Science
Microbook *Library of American Civilization*
Musicache
The Negro: Emancipation to World War I
Reports of Explorations in the Documents of the United States
    Government
Russian Revolutionary Literature

Slavery: Source Materials and Critical Literature
Source Materials in the Field of Theatre
Travels in the Old South
Travels in the West, Southwest, and Northwest
Underground Press Collection
Western Americana
Witchcraft in Europe and America

Each of these sets may contain hundreds or thousands of publications. And there are many other collections; especially noteworthy are the complete sets of books published within various countries up to a certain date; the various exhaustive collections of literature, drama, or poetry for particular countries; and many collections of national and international government publications. A closer look at three of the above sets will give some indication of the riches that are covered.

Goldsmiths'-Kress Library of Economic Literature.   Segment One of this huge collection contains approximately 30,000 books printed before 1801; Segments Two and Three, in progress, will contain books published from 1801–1850 and serials/periodicals. (Segment Two will include another 30,000 titles.) The *Guide* to the set suggests its range:

> In addition to the standard, well-known works used in studying the history of economics and business, the microfilm library contains unusual and exceedingly rare items which offer unique possibilities for comparative and cross-cultural research in the history of economic thought. Moreover, the collection is extremely rich in materials on political and social history in particular, and on history in general. Individual works are seldom confined to a single academic discipline, as the period antedates modern academic specialization. The micropublication thus constitutes a major research source for all social scientists and historians, as well as for economists.

Among the subjects covered are mercantilism, agriculture, emigration, usury, European colonial expansion, slavery, demography in eighteenth-century England, the textile industry, socialism, trade unionism, piracy, dietary habits in various European countries, early business and technical education, commerce in Italy, penology, trade manuals, numismatics, the economy of eighteenth-century Scandinavia, Irish-English relations, social conditions, population, transport and transport technology, and even theology. The materials are in the range of European languages.

Human Relations Area Files. This is a huge, ongoing collection of source materials (mainly published books and articles, although some unpublished manuscripts and reports of field research are included) for the worldwide, comparative, cross-cultural study of human behavior and society as represented in over 300 cultures. It is useful to students of anthropology, sociology, psychology, politics, literature, home economics, comparative religion, art, and agricultural development—and for anyone else who wishes to compare the perceptions, customs, social institutions, values, beliefs, and daily life of all peoples of the world, past and present. The microfiche source documents are arranged in over 300 groups, each representing a different culture; and each culture is then analyzed, insofar as the documentation permits, into some 600 categories (e.g., mortality, recorded history, food production, architecture for various functions, humor, entertainment, trial procedures, recruitment of armed forces, old age dependency, sexual practices and norms, views on abortion, drug use, division of labor by sex, sanitary facilities, power development, interpersonal relations, art, religion, political organization, etc.). Within each category is found, on microfiche, all relevant descriptive documentation drawn from over 5000 sources. (Foreign-language materials are translated into English.) The standardization of categories under each culture allows for ready comparisons of information, which in many cases can be statistically significant. The cultures are listed in the accompanying publication *Outline of World Cultures,* while the subdividing categories are listed in *Outline of Cultural Materials.*

Microbook *Library of American Civilization.* According to the guidebook that accompanies this set,

> It contains more than 6,500,000 pages of materials relating to all aspects of American life and literature, from the beginning to the outbreak of World War I. Included are pamphlets, periodicals, documents both public and private, biographies and autobiographies of persons both known and obscure, fiction and nonfiction, poetry, collected works and papers, material of foreign origin relating to America, and many rare books not generally available.

It is essentially a full historical library of approximately 10,000 books in a filing cabinet, covering early exploration, colonial history and records, politics and government, military history, foreign policy, constitutional history, law and law enforcement, the frontier, the South, local history, Indians and other minorities, agriculture, the city, business, labor, religion, education, reform, intellectual history, science and technology, literature, the various useful and performing arts, architecture, manners and customs, and so on. There are separate author, title, and subject index volumes.

Most of the other microform sets are equally amazing. Two important points to remember, however, are:

1. In most cases *none* of the individual items within a collection will be separately listed in the library's card (or computer) catalog. The *only* indication in the card file will be a record of the printed *Guide* that accompanies the set and lists its contents; it will usually be found under the heading "[Subject]—Bibliography." If you miss this one entry, you will in effect miss all of the possibly thousands of relevant sources in the collection.

2. For the time being at least, none of the individual items within these collections is recorded in the *National Union Catalog* or OCLC systems (although the *Guide* volumes accompanying the sets may be). If you are looking for a particular book or serial and do not find a nearby library that owns it recorded in these systems, it is still possible that a local library may own the item as part of one of these massive microform sets. This is especially true if the desired work is a British or American book, serial, or government document published before the current century.

One microform collection that is not listed in Dodson's *Guide* but which should be of interest to any serious researcher is the aggregate set of approximately 650,000 American doctoral dissertations available from University Microfilms International. The only library in the country that owns all of them is the Library of Congress; individual titles, however, can be purchased directly from UMI through the procedure explained in the index to the set, called *Comprehensive Dissertation Index*. These studies provide a staggering array of knowledge in all areas of inquiry; and, too, they usually contain excellent bibliographies.

Another equally amazing set not in Dodson's *Guide* is the collection of National Technical Information Service (NTIS) reports. Again, the Library of Congress is the only facility that owns all of them; however, individual titles may be ordered directly from NTIS (see below).

Government Documents

The term "document" is synonymous with "publication"; it can refer to just about any form of printing including monographs, magazines, reports, pamphlets, broadsides, maps, prints, photographs, posters, kits, and so on. Also included in government documents are many finding aids and reference sources such as catalogs, indexes, directories, dictionaries, and bibliographies.

The U.S. federal government—with whose publications this section is concerned—also produces films, sound recordings, audiovisuals, and microforms.

The range, variety, and depth of coverage of these materials are amazing. They are particularly thorough in scientific and technical areas, and in all the social sciences, but there are surprising contributions to the humanities as well (e.g., from the Smithsonian Institution, the Library of Congress, and the National Endowment for the Humanities). In using government documents, you can ask almost the same questions—and expect to find answers—as you can in using the more well-known research tools.

Since it is impossible to speak systematically of the range of these materials, let me offer a menu of titles, simply to suggest some of the possibilities available:

Camper's First Aid
Miro: Selected Paintings
Basic Electricity
A Guide to Budgeting for the Family
Family Therapy: A Summary of Selected Literature
The Educational System of Switzerland
The Income Tax Treatment of Married Couples and Single Persons
Nuclear Powerplant Safety After Three Mile Island
Midlife Women: Policy Proposals for Their Problems
Occupational Outlook Handbook
How Basic Research Reaps Unexpected Rewards
Marijuana: A Study of State Policies and Penalties
Handbook of North American Indians
Beekeeping in the United States
Growing Vegetables in the Home Garden

Sex and the Spinal Cord Injured

Annotated Bibliography and Subject Index on the Shortnose Sturgeon, Acipenser Brevirestrum

Solar Hot Water Handbook

Interlocking Directorates Among the Major U.S. Corporations

Delightful Places: A Book Tour of English Country Houses and Gardens

Great Houses and Their Treasures: A Bibliographic Guide

A Comprehensive Review of the Commercial Oyster Industries in the United States

Guide to High Speed Patrol Car Tires

The Murals of Harold Weston

The Effects of Nuclear War

The Role of Women in the Military

Photographer's Mate [training manual]

Journalist [training manual]

Low-Cost Wood Homes for Rural America: Construction Manual

Building the Solar Home

A Descriptive List of Treasure Maps and Charts in the Library of Congress

Nutritive Value of Foods

The Calibration of a Burn Room for Fire Tests on Furnishings

Cantonese: Basic Course [also similar books for French, German, Spanish, Swahili, Hebrew, Sinhala, Greek, etc.]

Diplomatic Hebrew

What You Should Know About Smoke Detectors

Survival, Evasion, and Escape

Poisonous Snakes of the World

Drug Paraphernalia

Project MKUltra, the CIA's Program of Research in Behavior Modification

Economic Problems of Rural America

Science Policy Implications and Energy: The Potential Savings of Different Modes

Radiologic Technology

Study and Teaching Opportunities Abroad

A Barefoot Doctor's Manual

Fundamentals of COBOL: Programmer's Reference

A Study of Lumber Used for Bracing Trenches in the United States

Harpsichords and Clavichords
Wildlife Portrait Series
U.S. Directory of Federal Regional Structure
The Global Report 2000 to the President
Rape Victimization in 26 American Cities
The Ship's Medicine Chest and Medical Aid at Sea
A Report on the U.S. Semiconductor Industry
The Star of Bethlehem [LC bibliography]
A Reader's Guide for Parents of Children with Mental, Physical,
*   or Emotional Disabilities*
Children's Literature: A Guide to Reference Sources
Occupational Diseases: A Guide to Their Recognition
The Back-Yard Mechanic
The Translation of Poetry
The Social and Economic Status of the Black Population in the U.S.:
*   An Historical View, 1790–1978*
Family Folklore: Interviewing Guide and Questionnaire
Homebuyer's Information Package: A Guidebook for Buying and
*   Owning a Home*
Angler's Guide to the United States Atlantic Coast [also *Pacific Coast*
*   volume*]
Marine Life Posters
Fifty Birds of Town and City
Ducks at a Distance: A Waterfowl Identification Guide
Research on Sleep and Dreams
The Martian Landscape (with 3-D stereo viewer)
Washington Architecture 1791–1861
The Price of Death: A Survey Method and Consumer Guide for
*   Funerals, Cemeteries, and Grave Markers*
A Guide to the Study and Use of Military History
Climate Change to the Year 2000
Literary Recordings: A Checklist of the Archives of Recorded Poetry
*   and Literature in the Library of Congress*
Catalog of Federal Domestic Assistance
Standard Industrial Classification Manual (and *Supplement*)
A Study of Global Sand Seas
NOAA Diving Manual
Farm Structure: A Historical Perspective on Changes in the Num-
*   ber and Sizes of Farms*

Small Business Location and Layout

Drug Themes in Science Fiction

Career Opportunities in Art Museums, Zoos, and Other Interesting Places

Crime Scene Search and Physical Evidence Handbook

Raising a Small Flock of Sheep

Defining Death: A Report on the Medical, Legal, and Ethical Issues in the Determination of Death

For Women: Managing Your Own Business

Fermentation Guide to Potatoes

The Bark Canoes and Skin Boats of North America

Books That Help Children Deal With a Hospital Experience

How to Buy a Christmas Tree

How to Buy Surplus Personal Property from the Department of Defense

How to Sell to Government Agencies

Selling to the Military

How Trees Help Clean the Air

Report of the Commission on Obscenity and Pornography

Chinese Herbal Medicine

The Hammered Dulcimer in America

Many of these publications are themselves but the tip of an iceberg—whenever you find one document on a subject that interests you, you can usually figure that there are many others waiting to be discovered (see especially the *Subject Bibliography* series, described below). The Government Printing Office has published over 50,000 titles per year in recent years.

If you have not tried documents before, you almost have to make a leap of faith to start looking for them; but it is probable that you will be pleasantly surprised. (And students who use documents will almost invariably find that none of their classmates have found the same sources.)

A number of reasons account for the general neglect of government publications by academic and other researchers; let me extend a few points made at the beginning of this chapter.

- Although the government spends millions of dollars a year to publish these materials, it spends very little to advertise them. Some enterprising private companies republish documents for a wider audience—which is perfectly allowable, since virtually nothing printed by the Government Printing Office is copyrighted—but such efforts pick up only a fraction of what is available.

- Libraries that own collections of government documents often shelve them separately rather than integrate them into the general collections. This is done because the best access to documents is provided by their own special indexes, which are keyed to Superintendent of Documents (SuDocs) call numbers rather than Library of Congress numbers, and the two cannot be interfiled. The result is that you will not find documents through the two major avenues of subject access to the library's books—the card catalog and shelf-browsing. (And even in its own section a documents collection cannot be browsed very efficiently because the SuDocs scheme arranges items according to the agencies that produced them and *not* according to the *subjects* of the documents. This is the difference between an archival scheme of arrangement and a subject classification scheme.)

- Documents are not covered by the most commonly used indexes and catalogs.

- Documents are not sold in most bookstores, so even avid readers have little opportunity to become aware of their existence.

- Courses in government publications are not required in library schools. One result is that not all librarians are themselves aware of their potential. This is unfortunate for researchers, because you probably won't be referred to documents in the first place unless you chance upon someone with experience in using them.

There are two types of government documents collections: regional depositories and selective depositories. The regionals are required by law to receive and permanently retain copies of *all* federal documents available through the depository program. Selective depositories are just that—they can choose which categories of publications they wish to receive and can weed their collections. A directory of which depositories are in which cities—including where the regionals are located—is available in any public library.

Law school libraries are usually selective depositories, but they generally confine their selections to series of law-related materials and administrative decisions.

It is noteworthy for researchers that all depositories (including those at law schools) must admit the general public to their documents collections. The law that allows them to receive free federal publications carries the condition that access must be open to all; schools that permit only their own students to have access to the documents can lose their depository status.

For those who wish to undertake systematic research in U.S. government documents there are a variety of indexes that have different strengths and weaknesses, and must therefore be used in combination:

Monthly Catalog of U.S. Government Publications. The *MoCat* is the basic "umbrella" index to government documents, excluding NTIS reports (for which, see below). It is intended to be a complete list, with cumulated annual indexes, to all federal publications. Currently, it allows access through LC subject headings, titles, title key words, authors, and report/series numbers. For retrospective searches using this index it is useful to note the existence of a separate publication, the *Cumulative Subject Index to the Monthly Catalog of United States Government Publications 1900–1971* (Carrollton Press, 1973–1975). There is also a *Cumulative Title Index to United States Public Documents 1789–1976* (U.S. Historical Documents Institute) and a *Cumulative Personal Author Indexes to the Monthly Catalog of U.S. Government Publications 1941–1975* (Pierian Press). A cumulative approach through corporate author or agency name is provided by volumes 606–624 of the *National Union Catalog of Pre-1956 Imprints,* which has also been republished as a separate set. In addition, three companies (including Information Access, which produces *Magazine Index*) have recently marketed microfilm machines that cumulate all *MoCat* entries from either 1976 or 1978 to date, with monthly recumulations of the entire file; access is through author, title, agency, or LC subject headings (but not through key words). Several other indexes and catalogs for historical approaches are ably discussed in Joe Morehead's *Introduction to United States Public Documents,* 3rd ed. (Libraries Unlimited, 1983), which is the bible for document researchers. Richard J. D'Aleo's *FEDfind: Your Key to Finding Federal Government Information* (ICUC Press, 1982) is also quite good.

GPO Sales Publications Reference File (PRF). This monthly publication (with interim biweekly supplements) is a deck of microfiche cards that is, in effect, the "Books in Print" list for Government Printing Office publications. It allows access to documents through subject headings, titles, key words, key phrases, series, personal authors, SuDocs numbers, and GPO stock numbers. Although not as extensive in its coverage as the *Monthly Catalog,* it often provides listings that are more current.

CIS/Index (Washington: Congressional Information Service, Inc., 1970–   ; monthly with annual and five-year cumulations).   This is the most thorough index to all Congressional publications since 1970, including hearings, committee prints, and House and Senate reports and documents. It is especially useful because Congress has so many oversight interests and responsibilities that generate detailed studies; these investigations monitor all areas of U.S. society and world relations. Most people are aware, simply from newspaper coverage, of Congress's investigations of regulatory reform, military spending, social security problems, nuclear energy, and foreign policy, but the many hearings it conducts on smaller issues are underpublicized and underutilized. The value of hearings is that they usually assemble top experts and interested parties on all sides of an issue to testify on the current state of a problem and recommend specific courses of action. Often there is extensive documentary material appended. This kind of overview is not often available elsewhere. Some examples of recent hearings include:

Acid Rain
Use of Drugs During Pregnancy
Laser Technology—Development and Applications
Toxic Shock Syndrome
Parental Kidnapping
Elephants
Sex and Violence on TV
Child Sexual Abuse Victims in the Courts
Street People
Structure of the Solar Energy Industry
Americans Over 100
White Collar Crime in the Oil Industry
Panama Gunrunning
Severe Storms Research
Applications of Space Technology for the Elderly and Handicapped
Small Business Problems in the Marketing of Meat and Other Commodities

Environmental Effects of the Increased Use of Coal
Effect of Pornography on Women and Children
Food Safety: Where Are We?
Economic Implications of Bishops' Pastoral Letter on the American
    Economy
First Use of Nuclear Weapons

Retrospective coverage of hearings from 1833 to 1969 is provided
by the *CIS U.S. Congressional Committee Hearings Index;* of prints
from 1830 to 1969, by the *CIS U.S. Congressional Committee Prints
Index;* and of miscellaneous Congressional reports and documents from
1789 to 1969, by the *CIS U.S. Serial Set Index.* (Coverage of all three
from 1970 onwards is provided by the basic *CIS/Index.*) An additional
related set is CIS's *Unpublished U.S. Senate Hearings: Early 1800s
through 1964.* Any library that owns any of these indexes may also
own the corresponding microfiche set of all documents indexed.

Committee prints are particularly noteworthy as they are often in-
depth studies commissioned by Congress to provide an overview and
detailed analysis of particular subjects, many being written by the
Congressional Research Service of the Library of Congress.

Most of the investigative and background reports written by the
Congressional Research Service, however, are theoretically available
only to Members of Congress—or available to the public only through
requests directly to Congressional offices. Those picked up by the CIS
indexes are only a minority of the ones actually written. But another
publisher is acquiring and publishing the majority of these CRS reports
and issue briefs—University Publications of America—and its *CRS
Series* includes studies written by the Congressional Research Service
and its predecessor organization, the Legislative Reference Service,
since 1916. Supplements are added to the basic 1916–1974 set on an
annual basis.

American Statistics Index, or *ASI* (Washington: Congressional Information Service, 1974–   ; monthly with annual and five-year cumulations).   The 1974 edition of this index picks up statistics back to
the early 1960s. Statistics are the backbone of documents research
since the federal government either counts everything imaginable itself
or assembles figures from others who do. *ASI* provides detailed subject
access to *every* statistical table, list, or publication produced by the

government. Especially useful are its many category indexes (e.g., "By State," "By Industry," "By Occupation," "By Sex," etc.) that greatly facilitate finding comparative figures. Through *ASI* you can find answers to such questions as "How much advertising do Chicago TV stations sell?"; "How much of the coal used in U.S. coke plants comes from Fayette County, Pa.?"; "How many children of unemployed parents are on welfare in California?"; and "How many people are killed each year in bombing incidents and what are the motives behind such incidents?"[1] Almost any question that involves counting, pricing, or categorizing can be approached through this index.

CIS also produces two other similar indexes: *Statistical Reference Index* (1980–   ) and *Index to International Statistics* (1983–   ). The first is a wide-ranging index to statistics produced by nonfederal agencies such as state and municipal bodies, universities, trade and industry groups, think tanks, private pollster companies, and so on; the latter covers the statistical publications of international governmental organizations. As with the *CIS/Index,* any library that owns the *ASI, SRI,* or *IIS* may also own a corresponding microfiche set that provides the full text of the documents indexed; but remember that none of the fiche will be recorded in the library's card catalog. (*SRI* is especially useful to business researchers, as it often provides rankings of companies by name—such niceties appear less often in federal statistics.) The same publisher has recently come out with another microfiche set, too: *Current National Statistical Compendiums,* which includes the statistical yearbooks of eighty countries around the world.

Index to U.S. Government Periodicals (Chicago: Infordata International Incorporated, 1970–   ; quarterly with annual cumulations).   This is an ongoing multidisciplinary index by author and subject to articles appearing in about 170 periodicals published by the government, most of which are not covered by any other index. Its range of coverage includes everything from abortion to zoology, and anyone who uses the *Readers' Guide to Periodical Literature* or *P.A.I.S.* would find the *Index* useful in the same ways. It is another gold mine for students in particular, as they can safely assume that no one else in their class will use it. There is a companion set called *Current U.S. Government Periodicals on Microfiche,* available from Microfilming Corporation of America, which provides the full text of all articles indexed in the *IUSGP.*

Subject Bibliographies, SB-series (Washington: GPO). This provides an excellent short-cut in documents research. There are over 300 such bibliographies, each revised irregularly, each listing in one place a whole range of in-print government publications on a particular subject. Some of the topics covered are:

Aging
Anthropology
Architecture
Birds
Business and Business Management
Child Abuse and Neglect
Children and Youth
Civil War
Computers and Data Processing
Cookbooks and Recipes
Crime and Criminal Justice
Dentistry
Earth Sciences
Elementary Education
Engineering
Financial Aid to Students
Home Gardening of Fruits and Vegetables
How to Sell to Government Agencies
Juvenile Delinquency
Library Science
Maps, United States and Foreign
Medicine and Medical Science
Minorities
Motion Pictures, Film, and Audiovisual Information
Naval History
Nurses and Nursing Care
Photography
Poetry and Literature
Radiation and Radioactivity
Secondary Education
Solar Energy
Statistical Publications
Weather

Women
X-Rays
Zoology

There is a cumulative alphabetical list of all the subjects covered in the series; free copies of it are available from the Government Printing Office, which will also supply free copies of any of the individual bibliographies themselves.

Government Reports Announcements & Index (GRA&I) (Springfield, Va.: Department of Commerce, National Technical Information Service, 1946–   ; semi-monthly with annual cumulations).   Every year the federal government spends millions of dollars on grants and contracts for research; and each recipient of such funding is required to submit a report on the result of his or her work. The *GRA&I* is the overall index to these reports; it provides access by key word, personal author, corporate author, report number, and contract number. Each citation includes a full abstract of the work. (There is a corresponding database available through commercial systems, although it covers only from 1964 to date.)

NTIS studies cover virtually all subjects in science, technology, and social science fields; there is even some surprising coverage in the humanities, too. Since *70,000* new titles are added annually, you can expect to find a government-funded research report on just about anything. There are studies of air pollution, anchor chains, drug abuse, educational philosophy, food contamination, foreign military forces, Greenland's weather, junction transistors, leadership, personnel management, quark models, seafloor spreading, sex behavior, and the sociology of Peruvian squatter settlements. There is even a study of one of Lord Byron's poems—it was done as a master's thesis at the Air Force Institute of Technology; and since government money paid for it, it got picked up by NTIS.

These studies are a real boon to researchers who know enough to seek out the *GRA&I*, although it is the same material that occasionally calls forth a "Golden Fleece" award from Senator Proxmire. (In this connection, by the way, it is worthwhile to read *How Basic Research Reaps Unexpected Rewards,* GPO Stock No. 038-000-00436-6.)

The vast majority of NTIS reports are *not depository items* in documents collections, although the *GRA&I* itself is if the depository library chooses to receive it. If you need a copy of a particular report, you can either buy it from the National Technical Information Service or read it for free at the Library of Congress, which is the only library that owns a full set. The NTIS sales office is at 5285 Port Royal Road, Springfield, Va. 22161 (703 487-4650).

NTIS Title Index on Microfiche. This is a cumulated key-word-from-titles index to NTIS reports from 1964 to 1978, with annual supplements. The cumulation makes it easier to use than the *Government Reports Announcements & Index;* however, it does not include the abstracts that you will find in the *GRA&I.*

Energy Research Abstracts (Oak Ridge, Tenn.: Technical Information Center, 1976–   ; semi-monthly with semiannual and annual indexes). One of the most important uses of government documents these days is for the study of energy problems, and the *ERA* is an indispensable index to relevant scientific and technical reports, conference papers and proceedings, journal articles, patents, theses, books, and U.S. and foreign documents.

Joint Publications Research Service (JPRS) translations. This government agency publishes on microfiche thousands of English language translations of foreign newspaper and periodical articles and monographs; these are sent automatically to regional depository libraries and to any other depositories that choose to receive them. In 1981 alone about *86,000* translations were sent out. The ongoing index to these materials is called *Transdex* (1970/71–   ), which supersedes the earlier *Bibliography-Index to Current U.S. JPRS Translations* (1962–1970). It provides access by subject, author, country, and title of translated publication. The JPRS series is the largest ongoing translation project in existence; it covers all fields of knowledge and is particularly valuable for providing foreign perspectives on current events. (A similar service, on a smaller scale, is provided by the Foreign Broadcast Information Service, or FBIS, which translates foreign radio broadcasts. These are often more important than print sources in countries with low literacy rates. The *World Press Review,* which translates about twenty articles per month from around the world, and the weekly *Current Digest of Soviet Press* are also noteworthy for translations.)

JPRS translations, in their own way, rank with doctoral dissertations, Congressional hearings, and NTIS reports as incredible sources of information in any subject area. There is a very good chance that if you go out of your way to look into these collections you will be very pleasantly surprised; and there is a decent chance that you will be positively astonished. (Again, the Library of Congress is the only facility that owns a complete set of all four; but any regional depository will have a full set of the hearings and translations.)

The indexes listed above are the major avenues of access to government documents. Several other sources, however, deserve special mention.

- The federal government produces hundreds of films, slides, sound recordings, videotapes, and so on; and information about them can be obtained from the *1978 Reference List of Audiovisual Materials* and 1980 *Supplement* (both available from the GPO). Many other directories of government-produced audiovisuals can be found by looking in the *Monthly Catalog* under the heading "Audiovisual materials—United States—Catalogs," and by consulting the GPO *Subject Bibliography #73*. An excellent shortcut to this information may be found through the National Audiovisual Center (301 763-1896), which can identify which materials exist on whatever subject you're interested in.

- Several indexes produced by the government are the finest in their fields. Among these are the *Index Medicus* for medical literature; the *Bibliography of Agriculture* (published by Oryx Press from data provided by the National Agricultural Library); the two indexes from the Educational Resources Information Center, or ERIC, *Resources in Education* and *Current Index to Journals in Education;* and the Office of Personnel Management's *Personnel Literature,* an index to management-related articles.

- There are federally produced maps, charts, and aerial photographs of every section of the United States and many regions of the rest of the world. The wealth and detail of information in these materials is amazing, and is of use to anyone from campers and urban planners to genealogists trying to locate cemeteries. Two publications are particularly good for describing and illustrating the range of sources available, and for providing specific information of where to order copies. They are *Maps for America* (Revised ed.; GPO, 1981) and *Map Data Catalog* (GPO, 1980). The telephone reference service of the National Cartographic Information Center (703 860-6045) is also very useful; its specialists can acquaint you with the range of publications available for particular needs.

- The General Accounting Office is the primary Congressional watchdog that monitors the effectiveness of federal programs and expenditures; reports that its issues are an excellent complement to Congressional hearings and Congressional Research Service reports for supplying detailed studies of a vast range of current social, political, and scientific/technical subjects. Some of its recent reports have dealt with aircraft costs, consultants in government, construction costs, energy, fraud in federal programs, health care services, nuclear facility safety, product safety, program evaluation, public lands use, sexual exploitation of children, social security, juvenile offender rehabilitation, sewage disposals, weapons research, and wildlife conservation. These studies are particularly valuable because they are often the ones the Congressional decisionmakers themselves rely on. The ongoing index and abstracting service for these reports is called *GAO Documents;* it is published monthly by the General Accounting Office and has a cumulative annual index. If you first obtain the correct document numbers from this index for the reports that interest you, you can then get free copies from the GAO's documents service at (202) 275-6241.

- There are many researchers who, understandably, throw up their hands at the prospect of doing documents research in a library. Often it is the case, however, that those who balk at library research are whizzes at using the telephone to find out what they need. A very valuable but equally obscure guide to phone numbers and addresses of contacts for seekers of federal publications is the Defense Technical Information Center's *How to Get It— A Guide to Defense-Related Information Sources* (Revised January, 1989, from NTIS, #AD-A201 600/4/XAB). This 626-page directory lists contacts for all sorts of information in federal (and other) sources for reports, maps, pamphlets, documents, translations, and databases; it also tells you which forms are necessary for placing orders and gives information on costs, restrictions on access, and where particular types of reports or publications are indexed. It is especially good at explaining report numbers—if all you have is such a number, this guide will explain what it means and tell you whom to contact for a copy of the report.

- If you need to locate regional or other depositories for federal documents, or those for state, local, United Nations, or other international and foreign documents, there is a very good directory that will identify almost all such collections in the United States. This is the *Directory of Government Documents Collections and Librarians* (CIS, revised irregularly). Its arrangement is by state, then by city; and it has a particularly good index to special subject collections.

- One of the persistent problems that documents researchers have is that of trying to cite federal publications in a formal manner; most of the accepted style sheets don't adequately deal with documents. A recent manual, however, has finally solved the problem. It is *The Complete Guide to Citing Government Documents* by Diane L. Garner and Diane H. Smith (CIS, 1984).

It should be obvious at this point that few researchers would get very far into microforms or government documents (and the same could be said for special collections) if left only to the most widely known library indexes. What is required is that you actively seek out these collections. This will often mean making a leap of faith that the effort will be worthwhile; but you should give it a try anyway—the results may be spectacular.

Note

1. These examples come from some of the publisher's own promotional literature.

13

Reference Sources

Success in doing research is largely a matter of combining knowledge of techniques, knowledge of sources, and persistence. Researchers initiating inquiries will want to be aware of specialized encyclopedias and state-of-the-art review articles, and then of the several techniques that can be used to find more in-depth information:

- Controlled vocabulary subject heading searches in manual indexes
- Systematic browsing
- Key word searches in manual indexes
- Citation searches in manual indexes
- Searches using published bibliographies
- Computer searches (which can be done via subject headings, key words, or citations, but add the possibility [among other advantages] of post-coordinate Boolean combinations while [among other limitations] diminishing the possibilities of browsing)
- Talking to knowledgeable people.[1]

Each of these seven methods is potentially applicable in any subject area; each has distinct advantages and disadvantages; and each is capable of turning up information that cannot be reached by the other six. It is also advisable to remember that all computer searches have noteworthy limitations, that Boolean combinations of subjects can be accomplished by both online and noncomputer methods, and that particular treasures lie in special collections, government documents, and microform collections—which must be sought out more actively than other sources.

A knowledge of these few distinct techniques—and of the advantages and limitations of each—will enable most researchers to substantially increase the range and efficiency of their investigations in any subject area. Most scholars, unfortunately, do most of their research only on the basis of (1) looking at footnotes in sources they already have, (2) inefficient use of card catalogs, and (3) general browsing in the classified bookstacks of libraries. Those in the sciences tend to minimize even these pursuits, relying instead on talking to acquaintances. Very few researchers use catalogs and indexes efficiently because they routinely look under the wrong terms (confusing titles with subject headings or looking under generic rather than specific headings) and because they are familiar with only a small fraction of the range of indexes that exist. Reference to the outline of procedures sketched above, however, will enable most researchers to gain a simple overview of the *full range of options* available to them in any inquiry, and (I hope) also assist them to achieve a sense of "closure" in making estimates of what research remains to be done.

A knowledge of techniques, however, must be supplemented by a knowledge of sources. And this is facilitated by an understanding that the finding aids and reference materials in any field predictably tend to fall into certain *types* of publications that collectively form a kind of structure within the literature. (By "reference materials" I mean those that either point the way into the core literature contained in journals, reports, monographs, dissertations, etc.; or those that summarize, abstract, digest, or review it. Reference materials tend to be those forms of literature that are simply consulted rather than read from cover to cover.) A foreknowledge of this overall structure can alert you to distribute your efforts among a variety of paths of inquiry; it can also give you a sense of what further options are available if your initial attempts are unsuccessful in finding the desired information. The various "bones" within the reference structure are:

- *Encyclopedias.* Here the specialized sets devoted to particular subject areas are often more useful than the widely known general sets. The purpose of an encyclopedia is to summarize knowledge and to provide a starting point for more extensive research; it seeks to present an overview of a subject written in such a way that a nonspecialist can understand it. (Note that sets specialized in a particular *subject area* still tend to be written with a nonspecialist *audience* in mind.) An encyclopedia may be contrasted to a *treatise,* which attempts to provide all knowledge on a subject in a systematic (rather than an alphabetical) arrangement, and which may be written for specialists rather than laypeople.

- *Indexes and abstracts.* These serve to get you to the journal articles and research reports on your subject. Abstracts have the added advantage of providing brief summaries of the items they index, which enable you to do a quick literature review at an early stage of your research.

- *Computer databases.* These often contain the same information as conventional indexes and abstracts, but they offer the advantage of allowing you to comb through it in different ways (e.g., by key word searches and post-coordinate Boolean combinations).

- *Bibliographies.* These list publications on a particular subject, often including materials that are missed by online databases.

- *Guides to the literature.* These often provide a connected expository overview of the literature of a subject and its reference sources.

- *Review articles.* State-of-the-art reviews are somewhat like encyclopedia articles in attempting to provide an overall assessment of the state of knowledge of a particular subject. They are often longer, however; they are frequently written for an audience of specialists familiar with a particular jargon; and they often seek to provide comprehensive rather than simply introductory bibliographies.

- *Directories.* These serve to lead you to people, organizations, or institutions that are interested in and knowledgeable about particular subjects. They are especially valuable because they often provide the best key to the tremendous stores of knowledge that exist outside libraries.

- *Yearbooks.* These provide reviews and assessments of the most recent year's developments in a field.

- *Newsletters and loose-leaf services*. These provide daily or weekly updates of information in rapidly changing fields.

- *Handbooks and Almanacs*. These serve as compendia of a variety of miscellaneous information and are often especially good for tabular or statistical data.

- *Union lists*. These enable you to identify which libraries own copies of the particular publications you are seeking. (Some union lists exist in database form.)

Within several of these categories it is useful to distinguish further which sources are searchable by subject headings, by key words, or by classified subject-grouping arrangement. The *method* of searching involved will have a significant effect on the results that can be achieved.

Students within a particular discipline usually learn its reference sources from a particular list they are given to study. The result is that they often learn the individual trees very well without perceiving the arrangement of the forest or the variety of methods available for getting through it, whether by walking, riding, flying over, swinging from branch to branch, or burrowing underneath.

The training of reference librarians, on the other hand, is more from the top down than from the bottom up. They learn first the overall arrangement that can be expected in *any* forest—here the analogy is not perfect—and the various methods of moving around in it. They hold an overall set of *categories* of sources in mind, with a knowledge of several distinct methods of combing each category (e.g., "What this question requires is a bibliography arranged by a subject classification scheme rather than alphabetically by subject headings"; "What this question demands is an index that allows a key word approach rather than subject heading access"; "What this question requires is a database that allows citation searching coupled with post-coordinate limitations by key words"). Even though they may not know particular titles or file names within a subject area, they do know beforehand that they can *reasonably expect* to find certain *types* of sources within which they can *reasonably expect* to find certain *methods* of access available, each with its own advantages and disadvantages. They therefore usually understand the *full range of options* for finding information even on unfamiliar subjects; for this reason they can often provide material on a subject more efficiently than even full professors within the discipline. The librarians may not understand the content of the discipline; but they do understand the predictable systems and methods of *finding* the content, which is a distinct matter. And the study of what can be expected in the arrangement, categorization, storage, and retrieval of information is a discipline unto itself: it is called library and information science. Those who have not studied it formally should be very careful about assuming that they are doing fully efficient research "on their own," for there will almost always be more options in searching than they realize. The moral of the story is brief: the more you know of what your options are, the better the searcher you will be; but remember to ask for help because the probability is that you will miss something important if you work entirely on your own.

Librarians have three major aids that help them to exploit the internal structure of the information sources within any given field. The first can be considered the basic source; the other two, updates. They are:

1. *Guide to Reference Books,* edited by Eugene Sheehy (10th ed.; American Library Association, 1986). This volume, known as "Sheehy," is the reference librarian's bible. It enables a searcher to look up any subject field and find within it a definitive listing of virtually all its important reference sources arranged according to the types of literature. The citations provide full bibliographic descriptions of each source for exact identification, plus descriptive annotations. The overall arrangement of the volume is by broad subject groups, with an index by authors, titles, and subjects.

2. *Reference Sources* (Pierian Press, 1977–). This annual publication is a comprehensive list of reference sources in all fields published during the year. Beginning with the 1980 volume it is arranged alphabetically by LC subject headings, with indexes by author and title. It is most useful as an ongoing and regular update of the latest Sheehy edition.

3. *ARBA: American Reference Books Annual,* edited by Bohdan S. Wynar (Libraries Unlimited, Inc., 1970–). Each annual volume in this series presents a listing of all reference books published in the United States within the preceding year. The distinctive feature of the series is that it provides a detailed review of each work listed. Indexes are by author, title, and subject. *ARBA* thus serves

as another excellent update of Sheehy. Three five-year cumulative indexes (1970–1974, 1975–1979, and 1980–1984) have appeared since the beginning of the series, and these cumulations are themselves major guides to reference books. Some libraries keep them next to their Sheehy.

There is still another volume—a kind of "mini-Sheehy"—that every researcher should own. This is *Reference Books: A Brief Guide*, compiled by Marion V. Bell and Eleanor A. Swidan (Enoch Pratt Free Library, revised irregularly). It is an excellent brief list, with comparative and evaluative annotations, of the most important reference sources in all fields. Ordering information can be found in *Paperbound Books in Print*.

Researchers who have never seen a copy of Sheehy would be well advised to spend some time browsing through it. It is likely to alert you to the existence of so many good sources that, right there, you may start allowing yourself to ask questions you never thought could be answered. And it is the hallmark of a good researcher to start out by assuming that every question has its answer somewhere.

Note

1. Other techniques such as original observation and analysis, controlled experimentation, and statistical surveying or sampling are beyond the scope of this book. Research in manuscripts and archives is discussed in the Appendix.

Appendix
Special Cases

The sources discussed in this section have proven themselves useful in providing answers to many specialized questions. By no means are they the only materials available; others can be found by using the approaches discussed elsewhere in this book.

The special cases covered are:

Archives, Manuscripts, and Public Records
Author's Guides
Biography
Book Reviews
Business and Economics
Conference Proceedings
Consumer Product Evaluations
Current Awareness Sources
Films and Audiovisual Material
Genealogy and Local History
Illustrations, Pictures, and Photographs
Literary Criticism
Manufacturers and Products
Maps
Newspaper Indexes
Psychological and Educational Tests
Reports
Standards and Specifications

Statistics
Tabular Data
Translations

Archives, Manuscripts, and Public Records

It is useful to consider unpublished primary sources as falling into two classes: archives or manuscript collections that have been assembled in special historical repositories, and current sources that are still with the people or agencies that originally created or received the records. Both offer gold mines of historical and biographical information.

Research in archives or historical manuscript collections is unlike research in books or journal articles in libraries. The latter sources are comparatively well indexed and cataloged, and there is subject access to individual items. Not so with unpublished sources—there may be broad subject access to large groups of items, but not to individual papers or documents within the groups. A major reason for this is that most individual unpublished sources are simply not worth the time and expense it would take to catalog or index them fully, for most of them make sense only within the larger context of the other items they are stored with. The strategy of working with such materials involves four levels of searching:

1. Identifying which repositories have collections or archival manuscript materials that are relevant to your subject.

2. Determining if there is a separate repository guide that will give you an overview of the holdings of a particular repository you're interested in.

3. Finding out if that repository has an archival inventory or manuscripts register for a particular series of documents you wish to examine.

4. Browsing through the documents themselves, which will be grouped according to who wrote or received them, or which agency produced them—often regardless of what their subject may be.

At the first level several good sources will help you identify which collections exist. Philip M. Hamer's *A Guide to Archives and Manuscripts in the United States* (Yale University Press, 1961) is a standard source, listing about 1300 repositories and describing their holdings. It has an index of names and subjects. The National Historical Publications and Records Commission's *Directory of Archives and Manu-script Repositories in the United States* (National Archives, 1988) supplements but does not supersede Hamer. The *Directory* describes 4225 repositories, and reports minimally on another 335 for a total of 4560. It too has an index allowing name and subject access. The *National Union Catalog of Manuscript Collections* (Library of Congress, 1959–) is an annual listing of thousands of reported collections from all over the country; it also has name and subject indexes. Lee Ash's *Subject Collections* (Bowker, revised irregularly) is a subject guide to over 10,000 special library collections in the United States and Canada, and many of these include unpublished or manuscript materials. The Modern Language Association also publishes two relevant sources, John A. Robbins's *American Literary Manuscripts* (2nd ed., 1977), a directory of 2800 authors' papers in 600 repositories, and James Thorpe's *The Use of Manuscripts in Literary Research* (2nd ed., 1979), a handbook explaining problems of access and literary property rights. Philip C. Brooks's *Research in Archives* (University of Chicago Press, 1969; Midway reprint, 1982) is also good for an overview.

At the second level, the *Guide to the National Archives* (GPO, 1987) may serve as an example of a particular repository guide. This book describes the various Record Groups held by the Archives; these groups of government records are arranged not by subject but rather by agency or bureau. If you wish to find out which agencies' records have material on your subject, you must use some imagination in thinking how the federal government would have become involved with your area of interest—for, with very rare exceptions, there are no subject or name indexes to the records. For this reason alone you must work closely with the archivists, who have a good sense of what types of things can be found in the various agencies' documents. The same rule applies at other repositories: use the expertise of the staff as much as you can and be sure that they understand *clearly*—and not just in vague; general terms—what it is you are *ultimately* trying to research.

The third level of guide is that of the archival inventory or manuscript register; it is usually a typed finding aid that describes one particular collection with an introductory note followed by a listing of the parts of the collection down to the box or folder level (but rarely to the level of individual items within the boxes or folders). Most of these inventories and registers are themselves unpublished and are available only at the repository. Some noteworthy exceptions exist, however. The Chadwyck-Healy company is publishing sets of microfiche that reproduce several hundred finding aids from larger institutions in the United States. Part 1 of their *National Inventory of Documentary Sources in the United States: Federal Records* reproduces over 400 finding aids for collections in the National Archives, over 800 for collections in seven Presidential Libraries (Hoover through Ford), and over 200 in the Smithsonian Institution Archives. Part 2, the *National Inventory of Documentary Sources in the United States: Manuscript Division, Library of Congress,* reproduces 772 finding aids for collections in LC. (Note, however, that LC owns over 10,000 such collections.) Part 3, covering selected *State Archives, Libraries and Historical Societies,* and Part 4, *Academic Libraries and Other Repositories,* are in progress. University or large public libraries may own these microfiche sets; consulting them locally may help to clarify your research strategy and save valuable time when you finally visit the repositories you choose. (Chadwyck-Healy also publishes a similar microfiche set covering British manuscript collections, the *National Inventory of Documentary Sources in the United Kingdom.*)

As helpful as the archival inventories and manuscript registers may be, however, only at the fourth level of research—reading through the documents themselves—can you really know what is in a collection. Keep in mind that you cannot do archival or manuscript research quickly; you must be prepared for much browsing and many dead ends before you come to any nuggets. Plan your time accordingly.

If you plan to visit an archival or manuscript repository, it is especially important to read as many secondary or published sources as you can on your subject *before* you inquire into the unpublished sources. Since these are not cataloged or arranged by subject, you will have to have in advance a rather clear idea of what you're looking for in order to recognize it when you're browsing. (It is especially useful to know in advance the names of any people connected with your area of interest; names are easy to look for in the records.) If you are planning a research trip, it is a good idea to write to the archives in advance, stating what you are interested in and asking for suggestions on what to read before you come in personally.

And once you are at the repository and are looking through the boxes of manuscripts or documents it has, *it is absolutely essential that you replace any material which you photocopy in the correct box.* The individual papers are *not cataloged,* so if you misplace an item it is *permanently lost for other researchers.*

Research in current public records—those that are still with the agency that produced or collected them and not yet sent to an archives—is another very valuable avenue of inquiry for studying individuals, businesses, or government itself. The best guide to finding such records is *The Reporter's Handbook: An Investigator's Guide to Documents and Techniques* by John Ullman and Steve Honeyman (St. Martin's Press, 1983). It is a thorough discussion of what public records exist and what you are likely to find in them when investigating or "backgrounding" individuals, businesses, or institutions. It covers records such as those for taxes, professional licenses, elections, land holdings, corporations, bankruptcies, courts, labor, health and safety, law enforcement, health care, and education.

Another valuable source is the privately funded National Security Archive in Washington, D.C. This organization is systematically rounding up copies of thousands of documents retrieved from the federal government through Freedom of Information Act requests. It can be reached at 1-202-797-0882.

Other useful sources are discussed below in the sections on Biography, Business and Economics, and Genealogy and Local History.

Author's Guides

For academics seeking to have an article published, a useful source is an author's guide that will list the various journals within a discipline, describe the kinds of manuscripts they are seeking, specify the desired length of manuscripts, note style manual requirements, and give further information on refereeing, time before publication decision, publication lag time, copyright ownership, number of articles or reviews published per year, and so on. There are several such guides:

- *Author's Guide to Journals in Law, Criminal Justice & Criminology,* by Roy M. Mersky (Haworth Press, 1979).

- *Author's Guide to Journals in Library & Information Science,* by Norman D. Stevens (Haworth Press, 1982).

- *Author's Guide to Journals in Nursing & Related Fields,* by Steven D. Warner and Kathryn D. Schweer (Haworth Press, 1982).

- *Author's Guide to Journals in Psychology, Psychiatry & Social Work,* by Allan Markle (Haworth Press, 1977).

- *Author's Guide to Journals in Sociology & Related Fields,* by Marvin B. Sussman (Haworth Press, 1978).
- *Author's Guide to Journals in the Health Field,* by Donald B. Ardell and John Jones (Haworth Press, 1980).

One of the nice things about this Haworth Press series is that each volume also tells you where the various journals are indexed. But there are other guides as well:

- *Author's Guide to Accounting and Financial Reporting Publications,* by Richard J. Vargo (Rev. ed.; Harper & Row, 1981).
- *Author's Guide to Business Publications,* by William B. Wolf (University of Southern California, Research Institute for Business and Economics, 1967).
- *Author's Guide to Real Estate Publications,* by Jack P. Friedman (Texas Real Estate Research Center, Texas A & M University, 1979).
- *Author's Guide to Social Work Journals,* by Henry P. Mendelsohn (National Association of Social Workers, 1983).
- *A Compilation of Journal Instructions to Authors* (Dept. of Health, Education and Welfare, Public Health Service, National Institutes of Health, National Cancer Institute, 1979).
- *Library and Information Science Journals and Serials: An Analytical Guide,* compiled by Mary Ann Bowman (Greenwood Press, 1985).
- *MLA Directory of Periodicals: A Guide to Journals and Series in Languages and Literatures* (Modern Language Association, revised irregularly). This publication provides author's guide information for all of the 3000+ journals and series indexed in the *MLA International Bibliography.*
- *Medical & Scientific Author's Guide: An International Reference Guide for Authors to More than 500 Medical and Scientific Journals,* by Joan Barnes (Le Jacq Publishers, 1984).
- *Cabell's Dictionary of Publishing Opportunities in Business, Administration, and Economics,* edited by David W. E. Cabell, 2nd ed. (Cabell Publishing Co., 1981).

- *Directory of Publishing Opportunities for Teachers of Writing,* edited by William F. Woods (Community Collaborators, 1979).

- *Historical Journals: A Handbook for Writers and Reviewers,* by Dale R. Steiner (ABC-Clio, 1981).

- *Directory of Publishing Opportunities in Journals and Periodicals* (Marquis Academic Media, Marquis Who's Who, Inc., revised irregularly).

- *Journal Instructions to Authors: A Compilation of Manuscript Guidelines from Educational Periodicals,* edited by Barbara A. Parker (PSI, Incorporated, 1985).

- *Latin American Studies* (volume 1 of the *Academic Writer's Guide to Periodicals* series), compiled and edited by Alexander S. Birkos and Lewis A. Tambs (Kent State University Press, 1971).

- *East Europe and Slavic Studies* (volume 2 of the *Academic Writer's Guide to Periodicals* series), compiled and edited by Alexander S. Birkos and Lewis A. Tambs (Kent State University Press, 1973).

- *African and Black American Studies* (volume 3 of the *Academic Writer's Guide to Periodicals* series), compiled and edited by Alexander S. Birkos and Lewis A. Tambs (Libraries Unlimited, 1975).

The best time to submit an article to a scholarly journal is in the late Spring, in May or, ideally, April. The worst time is in September or October because editors are frequently inundated with submissions during these months. (Scholars who have spent their summer months working on articles all tend to submit them at the same time.) Other things being equal, January and early February are also bad times for submission, since another glut tends to follow semester breaks and end-of-year conference meetings.

Biography

Two excellent starting points for biographical information are the *Biography and Genealogy Master Index* (Gale Research, 1980) with its *Supplements,* and *Biography Index* (H. W. Wilson Co., 1946–   ).

The former is a cumulative index to more than five million biograph-ical sketches in over 600 current and retrospective biographical dic-tionaries, including scores of *Who's Who* publications. *Biography In-dex* is the largest ongoing index to biographical materials in books, pamphlets, and periodicals (and it currently covers more than 3000 of the latter).

The *Biography and Genealogy Master Index* also exists in two other versions: a microfiche set called *BioBase* and an online database called *Biography Master Index,* which is available as File 88 in the Dialog system (see Chapter 9).

The Chadwyck-Healy company has recently produced an alphabeti-cal index on microfiche called the *Anglo-American Historical Names Database;* it indexes all personal names in a number of sources, in-cluding 273 British and Irish biographical dictionaries published from 1840 to 1940, the *National Union Catalog of Manuscript Collections,* the *National Inventory of Documentary Sources in the United States,* and the *National Inventory of Documentary Sources in the United Kingdom* (see the above section on Archives, Manuscripts, and Public Records). And K. G. Saur, Inc., has produced the *American Bio-graphical Archive,* a microfiche set that cumulates in one alphabetical sequence the full text of biographical articles on 350,000 individuals taken from nearly 400 reference works. Other microfiche sets in the *Biographical Archive* series (current or in progress) cover Italian, Ben-elux, Scandinavian, French, East European, and Spanish/Portuguese/ Ibero-American sources.

Current Biography, an ongoing hard-copy series, is the best place to look for articles on people currently in the news; each article is accompanied by a photograph. The *New York Times Biographical Ser-vice,* which reproduces biographical articles from that paper, is some-what comparable.

The two largest quick-reference sources on American biography for historical coverage are the multivolume sets *Dictionary of American Biography* and *National Cyclopedia of American Biography.* The for-mer is the standard in the field; the second is especially good for pick-ing up noteworthy people (e.g., business executives, clergy) who are otherwise neglected by the history books. The *Cyclopedia* articles tend to be authorized or approved by the biographees themselves.

If these sources don't cover the individual you want, often the var-ious national or specialized subject encyclopedias pick up obscure people, as does the *Personal Name Index to the New York Times Index 1851–1974* and *1975–1979* supplement. Slocum's *Biographical Dictionaries and Related Works* (a bibliography of approximately 16,000 items) can alert you to many sources not covered by the *Biography and Genealogy Master Index.*

Directories are also frequently useful for information on people. Academics will certainly want to be aware of the annual *National Faculty Directory*, which locates colleagues although it does not provide sketches of them. City directories such as those published by the R. L. Polk Company can be used to find a surprising amount of information about a person. Among the questions they can often answer are: Is the individual married? If so, what is the spouse's name? If a widower, what was the husband's name? Who else lives at the same address? Who are the neighbors? What is the individual's occupation and where is he or she employed? Is the individual a "head of house" or a resident? Retrospective searching of old volumes can also indicate how long an individual has been employed at a job, what previous jobs or business associations were, how long the person lived at an address, who were previous neighbors, and so on. (Researchers who want to learn how to milk directories to the last drop should study pages 158–160 of Harry J. Murphy's *Where's What: Sources of Information for Federal Investigators* [Quadrangle/New York Times Book Company, 1976]; Murphy quotes a previous publication listing about 50 questions city directories can answer.)

Book Reviews

Each of the Wilson indexes (see Chapter 4) has a separate "Book Reviews" section, but there are also several other indexes specifically for such articles. Among them are *Book Review Digest* (1905–   ), *Book Review Index* (1965–   ), *Current Book Review Citations* (1976–   ), *Index to Book Reviews in The Humanities* (1960–   ), *Combined Retrospective Index to Book Reviews in Scholarly Journals 1886–1974*, and *Combined Retrospective Index to Book Reviews in Humanities Journals 1802–1974*. The ISI citation indexes (see Chapters 5 and 6) also pick up book reviews, as well as footnote citations to books and articles. *Book Review Digest* picks up reviews from only 70 periodicals; but, unlike the others, it provides abstracts from the texts of the reviews and not just bibliographic citations. Note that these sources are generally not the best ones for students who want scholarly criticisms of individual books (see below, Literary Criticism).

Business and Economics

Two books everyone in this field should be familiar with are Lorna Daniells's *Business Information Sources* (2nd ed., rev.; Berkeley: University of California Press, 1985) and Paul Wasserman's *Encyclopedia of Business Information Sources* (Detroit: Gale Research, revised irregularly). Daniells's book is organized into twenty chapters on a variety of broad concerns (e.g., Chapter 6: Industry statistics; 7: Locating information on companies, organizations and individuals; 8: Investment sources; 10: Management; 18: Marketing). Each chapter then provides an excellent overview of the specific research resources in its area, with evaluative annotations. This book is the bible for business reference librarians. Wasserman's *Encyclopedia,* on the other hand, is arranged by *specific* subjects (e.g., Bismuth Industry, Condominiums, Dental Hygienists, Economic Entomology, Financial Ratios, Gages, House Organs, Inheritance Tax, Location of Industry, Molasses Industry, Retirement, Solar Power, Sweet Potato Industry, etc.), and under each has a good list of sources, although without annotations. Both Daniells and Wasserman arrange their sources by types of literature (e.g., books, encyclopedias, bibliographies, handbooks, abstracts and indexes, periodicals, directories, online databases, etc.).

In locating information on individual companies it is very important to first make a distinction between those that sell stock and are *publicly owned,* those which are *privately owned* and don't sell stock to the public, and those that are *nonprofit* organizations. Another distinction to keep in mind is that information about a company can be of two types: what the company says about itself, and what others say about it. For the first type of information you will use such things as annual reports and filings with government agencies. For the second you will use commercially prepared research reports or articles in business (or other) magazines and newspapers. Business reference books tend to be excerpts or compilations of the first type, or indexes to the second type, or some form of combination.

The very best source of information on a public company is the annual 10-K report it is required to file with the Securities and Exchange Commission. This "disclosure" information, mandated by the Securities Act of 1933 and the Securities and Exchange Act of 1934, provides a remarkably detailed look at a company's finances and operations. There are a number of ways to obtain 10-K reports. Researchers in Washington, D.C., can visit the SEC Public Reference Room at 450 Fifth St. N.W., Room 1024; researchers elsewhere may be able to find a microfiche set of these reports called *Disclosure* at local university or public libraries. A third way is through a private company called Disclosure, Inc., which will send you a copy of any SEC report you want for a minimum fee of $10.00 (they'll tell you over the phone the exact cost in advance; prices are subject to change). Disclosure also provides free copies of some very useful booklets such as *A Guide to SEC Corporate Filings: What They Are, What They Tell You* and *List of SEC Filing Companies*. Their toll-free number is 1-800-638-8241. Researchers can also have some Disclosure reports printed immediately online through the Dialog computer system.

Other good sources of information about publicly owned companies are the annual reports they issue to stockholders. These can be obtained directly from companies; they are also available in a microfiche set that may be owned by local libraries.

Other sources in libraries can also supply quite a bit of information on public companies. Factual, objective information on companies that sell stock is available from two loose-leaf services, Standard & Poor's *Standard Corporation Records* and Moody's Investor Service's *Moody's Manuals*. The former exists only in loose-leaf binders and does not cumulate (i.e., outdated pages are discarded as new ones come in). Moody's loose-leaf service is similar; however, Moody's is backed by permanent, bound annual volumes of reports on companies, and these are useful for researching the history of a company. A third loose-leaf service, *Value Line Investment Service,* provides analytical and evaluative ratings of companies and advice on investment, which *S&P* and *Moody's* do not.

Private securities and investment firms also prepare reports on individual public companies. And, recently, the JA Micropublishing Company of Eastchester, New York, has started rounding up thousands of such reports from 40 such firms and publishing them annually on microfiche with an index called *CIRR/Corporate & Industry Research*

Reports Index. Again, both the index and the microfiche set may be available in local libraries. Another source of information on such reports is the weekly *Wall Street Transcript,* which provides excerpts of important studies; it is indexed in *Predicasts* (see below). A directory called *Findex,* published by Find/SVP in New York, is the largest listing of commercially prepared studies of particular companies, industries, or markets; it will give you price and ordering information, and it has a mid-year supplement.

The best information on privately owned companies may not be in libraries at all. Since they do not sell stock, they are not required to file information with the SEC. However, they *may* be required to file annual reports with the Secretary of State of the state in which they are incorporated; but not all states require, or enforce, the filing of such information. A very good source listing the whole range of which public agencies may have information on private (and other) companies is Washington Researchers' *How to Find Information About Companies.* The same organization also publishes two case studies of in-depth investigations of private companies; the first is entitled *Company Information: A Model Investigation* (a look at Perdue Farms); the other is *Finding Company Intelligence: A Case Study* (on MCI Airsignal). Both discuss the "how" of the research process as well as the "what" of the findings. The volume mentioned above in the Archives section, *Reporter's Handbook,* is also a very good guide to the range of public records available on a company.

Other excellent sources on private companies are Dun & Bradstreet Business Information Reports. These are not available in libraries; but you may be able to obtain a copy of the one you need through your local banker, as most banks subscribe to the D&B service for information on the creditworthiness of companies, or from D&B directly.

The R. L. Polk Company's annual city directories for many U.S. cities are often good for providing the names of officers of private companies.

For nonprofit corporations, the best source of information is the corporation's public-record tax return (Form 990), available from the Internal Revenue Service. (Note that only the tax filings of nonprofit companies are publicly available.) The IRS publishes a list of these companies called *Cumulative List of Organizations Described in Section 170(c) of the Internal Revenue Code of 1954;* it is annual with quarterly supplements, and it may be found in many local libraries. It is no more than a list of corporate names with the city and state of each, however, and offers no further information. To actually see the tax return of a listed company, you must send a request *in writing* to:

> Freedom of Information Reading Room
> Internal Revenue Service
> Dept. of the Treasury
> 1111 Constitution Ave. N.W.
> Washington, D.C. 20024

This agency will acquire a copy of the document you seek from one of the nine IRS Service Centers around the country, then contact you (by phone, if you desire) to let you know the cost of photocopying the form (currently $1.00 for the first page plus 15¢ for each additional page).

A second useful source of information on nonprofit organizations is the annual *Encyclopedia of Associations* from Gale Research; it lists and describes about 20,000 of them.

Additional information on all three types of companies—public, private, and nonprofit—may sometimes be found in articles that have appeared in the business periodical literature. The best indexes allow access by both subject and company name; they are *Business Index*, *Business Periodicals Index*, the *Wall Street Journal Index*, *Predicasts F&S Index: United States*, *Predicasts F&S Index: Europe*, and *Predicasts F&S Index: International*. For information on local companies it is advisable to check your local newspaper, many of which have published indexes (see below, Newspaper Indexes); and a telephone call to the editor of the Business Section of the newspaper may turn up leads that have not been published. You should also call your local public library; some of them index the local paper or keep files of clippings on local businesses. It is especially useful, too, to remember that the *Social Sciences Citation Index* covers about 200 business and economic journals—for the *SSCI* offers access by key words and footnote citations, not by subject headings. All these business indexes are likely to be in the larger local libraries.

If you are interested in a larger perspective on whole industries rather than just individual companies, the same indexes (especially the *Predicasts* sets) are useful. A better starting point, however, is a quarterly publication, Standard & Poor's *Industry Surveys*. Wasserman's *Encyclopedia* is also quite good.

There are numerous other indexes to business literature such as *Accountants' Index, Index of Economic Articles,* the ongoing index in *Journal of Economic Literature,* and the Office of Personnel Management's *Personnel Literature.* There are also scores of online databases in the field. A good introduction to computerized sources of business information is Andrew Garvin and Hubert Bermont's *How to Win with Information or Lose Without It* (Washington, D.C.: Bermont Books, 1980), which gives many concrete examples of what kinds of questions can be answered through online sources. (The book does have a noteworthy weakness, however: it shows no awareness at all of the limitations of computer searches.) Another good introduction to the various online sources is Marydee Ojala's *Business Management Bibliographic Databases & News Services* (Los Altos, Calif.: Databases Services, 1981). And Dialog Information Services will send you a free handout on "Company Information on Dialog," which describes about 30 databases available on their system, if you call their Marketing Department at 1-800-227-1927 (outside California) or 1-800-982-5838 (inside California).

Several business directories are especially noteworthy. The *Thomas' Register of American Manufacturers* provides a subject approach to companies' goods and *some* services; it's like a *Yellow Pages* for the whole country. For services rather than goods, however, other directories are preferable such as the *Consultants and Consulting Organizations Directory* (Gale Research, revised irregularly); the best listing of which directories are available is the *Directory of Directories,* also from Gale. The *D-U-N-S Accounting Service* is the largest single listing of companies' addresses (both public and private) in the United States; it can often save you the trouble of looking through many telephone books. The *Findex* directory, mentioned above, is the best list of published market research reports. (Another good source for the latter is the microfiche set of documents accompanying the *Statistical Reference Index;* it includes the full text of many market studies.) Numerous large cities throughout the United States and Canada, too, have a *Contacts Influential* directory listing local businesses in several ways: alphabetically by firm name, by Standard Industrial Classification (SIC) code, by market concentration, by ZIP code and street address, by key people, and by crisscross phone numbers.

An especially useful source for finding information on obscure (and other) companies is the supposedly annual *Ward's Directory,* which is in three volumes: *Largest U.S. Corporations, Private U.S. Companies,* and *Major International Companies.* The volumes on the United States provide both public and private company names, addresses, and phone numbers, the name of the chief executive of each, and rankings within SIC industries by sales and employee size. Access is alphabetical by company name, by ZIP code, or by SIC industry code. The *International Companies* volume provides a listing, with similar name-address-phone-executive officer information, for public and private companies by country ranked within SIC industries by sales size.

The Small Business Administration staffs a referral service that gives some help in extracting business or other information from the federal government, and from state agencies and private sources. The number for the SBA Answer Desk is 1-800-368-5855.

For job-hunters, the very best book to read is Richard Nelson Bolles's *What Color Is Your Parachute?* (Berkeley, Calif.: Ten Speed Press, revised irregularly). Robert J. Gerberg's *The Professional Job Changing System* (Parsippany, N.J.: Performance Dynamics, revised irregularly) is also quite good, especially in its advice on resumes and cover letters.

Conference Proceedings

The best indexes to these elusive sources are produced by the same company that offers the citation indexes; they are: *Index to Scientific and Technical Proceedings (ISTP),* 1978 to date; and *Index to Social Sciences and Humanities Proceedings (ISSHP),* 1979 to date. Each has several sections: a Category Index (general subjects), a Sponsor Index (agencies or societies that sponsor meetings), a Corporate Index (organizational affiliations of individual authors), a Permuterm Subject Index (key words from book titles and subtitles, conference titles, and titles of individual papers), an Author and Editor index, and a Meeting Locator Index (by country and city). They are published quarterly, with annual cumulations.

Another good source is the annual *Bibliographic Guide to Conference Publications* (1974–) from G. K. Hall.

For earlier years, use the *Directory of Published Proceedings* 1965–) and *Proceedings in Print* (1964–). The *National Union Catalog* is also very useful.

If none of these identifies the paper you want, the best thing to do is to consult the *National Faculty Directory, American Men and Women of Science,* the *Directory of American Scholars,* or various of the *Who's Who* type publications. These will usually enable you to locate the current address of the author of the paper in which you are interested, and you can then contact the person directly for a reprint. (Authors provide these routinely.)

Consumer Product Evaluations

A good source to start with is the annual *Consumer Reports Buying Guide Issue,* which provides rankings of specific products and comparison information in all areas from autofocus cameras and cars (including used cars) to stereo equipment and videocassette recorders. Food items are included, too, and brand names are rated. (Copies are available in public libraries and local bookstores.) Another good source is the hardcover *American Buys: The Index to Product Evaluations* from Information Access Corporation. It cumulates the indexing of consumer and product information from 400 magazines, plus the *New York Times, Christian Science Monitor,* and *Wall Street Journal.* Unlike the *Buying Guide,* it does not itself summarize comparative information; it gives you citations to articles that provide the information. Information Access also has a loose-leaf supplement called *Product Evaluations* that is a companion to the microfilm *Magazine Index.* It gathers together, with monthly updates, the citations to consumer articles in those same 400 magazines.

Another good ongoing index is *Consumer Index to Product Evaluations and Information Sources* (quarterly with annual cumulations, 1974–); it covers about a hundred periodicals.

Sometimes whole books are published that compare and rate particular types of products, and these can be identified through *Subject Guide to Books in Print, Paperbound Books in Print,* and *Subject Guide to Forthcoming Books.*

Current Awareness Sources

Libraries that offer computer search services also offer a ''Selective Dissemination of Information'' (SDI) service, which means that you

can have a particular search strategy stored in the computer and automatically run against new update files as they come into the databases.
The result will be a bibliography tailored to your specifications, usually every month, alerting you to new publications. Another source
researchers should be aware of is the *Current Contents* series from the
Institute for Scientific Information. There are seven different *Current
Contents* journals, each with a subtitle denoting its subject area:

> *Agriculture, Biology & Environmental Sciences*
> *Arts & Humanities*
> *Clinical Practice*
> *Engineering, Technology & Applied Sciences*
> *Life Sciences*
> *Physical, Chemical & Earth Sciences*
> *Social & Behavioral Sciences*

Each of these is a weekly publication that reproduces the Table of
Contents from each of hundreds of journals within its subject area.
They're great for browsing if you want to find the *most* recent articles
in your field—the ones that have not yet been picked up by the conventional journal indexes.

There are also a number of yearbooks in various subjects that are
useful in updating one's knowledge; these can be identified through
Irregular Serials and Annuals and through the reference sources listed
in Chapter 13.

Films and Audiovisual Material

For educational materials there are two especially good indexes. One
is *Educational Film Locator* (Bowker, 1980) which lists about 200,000
films with locations of owner institutions; the other is a group of sources
known collectively as NICEM indexes. The National Information Center for Educational Media publishes separate indexes to the following:

> Educational Films
> Educational Audio Tapes
> Educational Video Tapes

8mm Motion Cartridges
Educational Overhead Transparencies
Educational Filmstrips
Educational Slides
Black History (multimedia)
Health and Safety Education (multimedia)
Psychology (multimedia)
Vocational and Technical Education (multimedia)

These provide subject and title access to the materials, plus addresses of producers and distributors. There is also a separate *Index* to producers and distributors.

Two government publications of particular interest are the National Audiovisual Center's *Reference List of Audiovisual Materials Produced by the United States* Government (1978 with 1980 supplement; *Quarterly Update* listings thereafter); and the GPO's *Subject Bibliography* #SB-073, *Motion Pictures, Films, and Audiovisual Information* (revised irregularly) that lists, among other things, catalogs of films available from the various federal agencies. (Both the *List* and the *Subject Bibliography* are available from the Government Printing Office.) The National Audiovisual Center can also be reached by telephone (1-302-763-1896; or 1-800-638-1300 for orders); its staff can tell you what government-produced A-V material exists on whatever subject interests you.

The largest overall index of theatrical films is *The Motion Picture Guide,* a multivolume guide to releases from 1927–1984, compiled by Jay Robert Nash and Ralph Ross (Chicago: Cinebooks, 1985). It lists 25,000 films with cast and production credits, and videocassette availability.

Genealogy and Local History

The best two books for genealogists to start with are Val D. Greenwood's *Researcher's Guide to American Genealogy* (Genealogical Publishing Co., Inc., 1978), which you should read completely before you do anything else; and *The Source: A Guidebook of American Genealogy,* edited by Arlene Eakle and Johni Cerny (Ancestry Publishing

Co., 1984), which provides the most extensive overview of what sorts of historical records exist on people, and where they are. And there are five other books that you should at least browse through:

- *American & British Genealogy and Heraldry,* 3rd ed., compiled by P. William Filby (New England Historic Genealogical Society, 1983).
- *Genealogical Research: Methods and Sources,* edited by Milton Rubincam and Ken Stryker-Rodda (2 vols.; American Society of Genealogists, 1980 & 1971).
- *The Handy Book for Genealogists,* edited by George B. Everton, Sr. (Everton Publishers, revised irregularly).
- *Genealogical Source Handbook* (by George K. Schweitzer (Schweitzer, 1979).
- *Search & Research* by Noel C. Stevenson (Deseret Book Co., 1977).

Two books with a focus on the Washington, D.C., area are also noteworthy. Colleen Stone Neal's *Lest We Forget: A Guide to Genealogical Research in the Nation's Capital* (Annandale Stake of the Church of Jesus Christ of Latter-Day Saints, 1982) describes in considerable detail the four main genealogical collections in the area: the National Archives, the Library of Congress, the Daughters of the American Revolution (DAR) Library, and the National Genealogical Society Library. It tells you clearly what you can expect to find in each, where the material is located in each, and what procedures are necessary to retrieve it. Another source especially useful for those who can visit D.C. is the new edition of *Guide to Genealogical Research in the National Archives* (GPO, 1982).

Two good genealogy courses are offered every year in Washington. The first is a week-long program entitled "Genealogical Research: How to Do It" held at the Smithsonian Institution; the second is a two-week "National Institute on Genealogical Research" offered at the National Archives. The Smithsonian course is preferable for beginners; it is a first-rate introduction to the range of sources and techniques available to genealogists, and its instructors speak from a vast fund of experience and anecdote (some of them also teach at the Archives' "Institute"). For information on the next scheduling of the course, contact the Selected Studies Seminars office at the Smithsonian (1-202-357-2475); and for the Archives program contact their Education Division (1-202-523-3298). (One of the interesting things you will learn in these courses is that published genealogies are the *least* trustworthy sources a researcher can use.)

An interesting sideline by which genealogists can enrich their understanding of the past is through the study of the history of neighborhoods and of individual buildings or sites. One especially noteworthy source is *Fire Insurance Maps in the Library of Congress: Plans of North American Cities and Towns Produced by the Sanborn Map Company* (Library of Congress, 1981). LC has a huge collection of these maps—623,000 covering 10,000 American cities and towns—and they are of interest because they can tell you who has previously owned the land on which you live, where your ancestors lived in the given city at the time of the map (some cities had as many as seven maps published at different times), how many rooms each building had, the number of windows, the kind of roof, and the materials the walls were made of. You can use them to identify which businesses were located in a community (when and exactly where), the location and denomination of churches, and where the groceries, banks, hotels, and saloons were. In conjunction with LC's collection of city directories these maps can provide you with an astonishing window on the everyday life of the past and endless opportunities for genealogical detection and deduction.

Illustrations, Pictures, Photographs

The *Library of Congress Subject Headings* system has several standard subdivisions that are useful for finding pictures in books; among them are:

[Subject heading]—Pictorial works
        —Caricatures and cartoons
        —Illustrations
        —Description—Views [for cities and smaller subdivisions]
        —Description and travel—Views [for regions larger than cities]

The Wilson indexes also note whether or not a journal article is accompanied by illustrations. And there are several one-volume indexes specifically for illustrations or reproductions of paintings, among them *Illustration Index* (Scarecrow, 1973), *Index to Illustrations* (Faxon, 1966), and *Index to Illustrations of the Natural World* (Gaylord, 1977). Both UNESCO and the New York Graphic Society publish catalogs of commercially available reproductions of paintings. The specialized encyclopedias are also frequently valuable for pictures.

Literary Criticism

Usually the best way to locate criticisms of a particular literary work—and sometimes the only efficient way—is to first find a bibliography of works about the particular author and then check its index. For example, a student who wants to find a close reading of John Donne's Holy Sonnet #10 ("Death Be Not Proud") could do so by first looking in the card catalog under "DONNE, JOHN, 1572–1631—BIBLIOGRAPHY." This would alert him to the existence of John R. Roberts's *John Donne: An Annotated Bibliography of Modern Criticism, 1912–1967* (University of Missouri Press, 1973), the index of which lists several close readings of this one sonnet.

Numerous specific sources can serve as an alternative to finding a full bibliography on one author (although the latter are becoming amazingly numerous). The standard bibliography of English literature is the *New Cambridge Bibliography of English Literature* (5 vols.: Cambridge University Press, 1969–1977). This lists the various editions and biographies of each author, plus critical works. It may not list criticisms of each individual work of an author, however; nor will it tell you which is the standard edition, the best biography, or the most worthwhile criticism. This shortcoming is remedied by F. W. Bateson and Harrison T. Meserole's *A Guide to English and American Literature* (3rd ed.; Longman, 1976). Bateson is the former chief editor of the *Cambridge Bibliography;* what he and Meserole do is tell you, for each author, what is the best scholarly edition of the works, the best biography, and the best overall criticism. This is very helpful for graduate students, but less so for undergraduates who want detailed criticisms of individual works.

For the latter purpose (assuming that individual bibliographies have already been checked), such compilations as the following are useful:

- *Poetry Explication: A Checklist of Interpretation Since 1925 of British and American Poems Past and Present* (G. K. Hall, 1980)
- *American and British Poetry: A Guide to the Criticism 1925– 1978* (Swallow Press, 1984)
- *English Novel Explication* (Shoe String Press, 1973) and *Supplements*
- *The Continental Novel: A Checklist of Criticism in English 1900– 1966* (Scarecrow, 1968)
- *The Continental Novel: A Checklist of Criticism in English 1967– 1980* (Scarecrow, 1983)
- *The Contemporary Novel: A Checklist of Critical Literature on the British and American Novel Since 1945* (Scarecrow, 1972)
- *The American Novel: A Checklist of Twentieth Century Criticisms on Novels Written Since 1789* (2 vols.; Swallow Press, 1961– 1970)
- *Articles on American Literature 1950–1967* (Duke University Press, 1970) and *Articles on American Literature 1968–1975* (Duke University Press, 1979)
- *Dramatic Criticism Index* (Gale Research, 1972)
- *Drama Criticism* (vols. 1 and 2; Swallow, 1966–1971)
- *Modern Drama: A Checklist of Critical Literature* (Scarecrow, 1967)
- *European Drama Criticism 1900–1975* (2nd ed.; Shoe String, 1977)
- *American Drama Criticism: Interpretations 1890–1977* (2nd ed.; Shoe String, 1979), and *Supplement* (1984)
- *Twentieth Century Short Story Explication* (3rd ed.; Shoe String, 1977) and *Supplement* (1980)
- *American Short Fiction Criticism and Scholarship 1959–1977: A Checklist* (Swallow Press, 1982)
- *Magill's Bibliography of Literary Criticism* (4 vols.; Salem Press, 1979) (This covers world literature.)

- *Black American Writers Past and Present: A Biographical and Bibliographical Dictionary* (2 vols.; Scarecrow, 1975).

Each of these is arranged by author and then subdivided by individual work, listing particular criticisms of each work. Alan R. Weine and Spencer Means' *Literary Criticism Index* (Scarecrow, 1984) is a cumulative index to 86 such bibliographies of criticisms.

Two sources that provide actual critical articles (not just bibliographic citations) on a wide variety of literary works are Magill's *1,300 Critical Evaluations of Selected Novels and Plays* (4 vols.; Salem, 1978) and Magill's *Survey of Contemporary Literature* (rev. ed., 12 vols.; Salem, 1977). These articles, however, are generally only one to three pages long. The *Survey* is updated by *Magill's Literary Annual* (Salem, 1977–   ).

One of the very best shortcuts to critical articles on major literary works is through the Prentice-Hall *Twentieth-Century Interpretations* series. Look in your library's card catalog under the title *Twentieth Century Interpretations of [Title of work]*. (Within the brackets you can enter such titles as *A Farewell to Arms, The Crucible, Doctor Faustus, Gray's Elegy, Julius Caesar, Moby Dick, Oedipus Rex, Pride and Prejudice*, etc.) There are about 90 volumes like this, each about 120 pages long, and each presenting an excellent collection of recent scholarly analyses. This shortcut doesn't always work; but when it does the results are quite good, and you probably won't have to do any further digging.

Another comparable series is Prentice-Hall's *Twentieth Century Views*. These tend to have titles of the format *[Name of author]: A Collection of Critical Essays*. The best entry into the contents of the series is an obscure but remarkably useful volume entitled *Reader's Index to the Twentieth Century Views Literary Criticism Series, Volumes 1–100* (Prentice-Hall, 1973). This book reproduces the index pages from the end of each volume in the series. It thus offers an excellent way to find articles on *particular topics* connected with authors (as opposed to particular works), such as "Negative capability in Keats," "Inscape and instress in Hopkins," "Irony in Mann," and "Puritan influences on Hawthorne." In a sense, you can use this compilation of indexes to do Boolean combinations of "specific topic and specific author" without having to use a computer.

The largest overall index to journal articles and books on all aspects of world literature is the Modern Language Association's annual *MLA International Bibliography;* there is a corresponding database available through the Dialog system (see Chapter 9). Other annual bibliographies devoted to particular literary periods, however, (e.g., Romantic Movement, Eighteenth Century) are more exhaustive within their own spheres; these are listed in Sheehy (cf. Chapter 13), in Bateson's *Guide,* in Richard Gray's *Serial Bibliographies in the Humanities and Social Sciences* (Pierian Press, 1969), in William Wortman's *Guide to Serial Bibliographies for Modern Literatures* (MLA, 1982), and in *Bibliographic Index.*

Perhaps the most important thing for an undergraduate to keep in mind when doing an analysis of a literary work, however, is that quite possibly no research at all is required, or even desired, by the professor. Often the purpose of such assignments is to stretch your analytical powers rather than your research abilities. Another problem with critical articles is that—as most graduate students in English will tell you— much of what you find simply won't be worth reading. And few things are more frustrating to a student than expending a lot of time and energy on research and getting only mediocre or off-target articles as a result. The time involved would often be more profitably and efficiently spent in devising your own analysis—for by going in that direction you can often have your paper completely written and typed while your colleagues are still compiling notes in the library.

Manufacturers and Products

The best national directory in this field is the annual *Thomas' Register of American Manufacturers,* which is a subject index to products and some services, giving supplier-company names, addresses with ZIP codes and phone numbers. There are also directories of manufacturers for individual states, for individual industries (e.g., paper, textiles), for international and overseas companies (e.g., *Kelly's Manufacturers and Merchants Directory, Jaeger & Waldmann International Telex Directory, Bottin International Business Directory*), and for particular foreign countries. Possibly the most useful sources for researchers, however, are the ones that are apt to be overlooked simply because they're so obvious: the *Yellow Pages* for various cities. (Note that the larger volumes use a controlled vocabulary for their subject headings—*and that a detailed index with cross-references is in the back of the volume.*)

Remember, too, that most large public libraries systematically collect phone books and yellow pages from all over the country. Some may have a subscription to a service called *Phonefiche,* from Bell & Howell, which reproduces these directories on space-saving and durable microfiche.

Maps

For people who want to order maps or aerial photographs of particular areas, two government publications (both available from the Government Printing Office) are outstanding. These are *Maps for America* and *Map Data Catalog.* A GPO summary of *Maps for America* is quite accurate: "The primary objectives of this volume are to inform the map user of the meaning of lines, color, images, symbols, numbers, captions and notes that appear on maps; the possible errors and anomalies affecting the reliability and interpretation of maps; the different kinds of maps and map data; the various sources of maps and related information." In other words, if you read this book you will enable yourself to ask many more questions—and expect to get answers from maps and photos—than if you hadn't. And that is the key to being good researcher. The second volume illustrates the various map and air photo products available from both government and private agencies, tells you what uses they have, explains the scope or geographic coverage available, and gives specific information on ordering copies (e.g., how to get color air photos from NASA aircraft and Skylab photos of major U.S. cities).

If you are confused about what sorts of map products are available, and where they can be found, you can call the National Cartographic Information Center for help (1-703-860-6045).

A noteworthy book for both consumers and scholars is *Kister's Atlas Buying Guide* by Kenneth F. Kister (Oryx Press, 1984), which compares and evaluates more than a hundred general and world atlases currently available in the United States and Canada.

Two loose-leaf services that may be available in local libraries are *Maps on File* and *Historical Maps on File,* both from the Follett Li-

brary Book Company. Each contains over 300 copyright-free black-
and-white maps intended for easy photocopying.

Newspaper Indexes

The complete run of the *New York Times* is indexed back to 1851;
most academic libraries own at least the more recent years of the *Index*
plus a microfilm set of the newspaper itself. Similarly, the *Times* of
London is indexed from 1790 to date, and microfilm of the paper is
widely available. The *Wall Street Journal* is indexed from 1959 to
date.

You can often use the *New York Times Index* to gain some access
into other papers that do not have their own indexes. Through it you
can often find the dates of relevant events, and use that time-frame to
narrow your search to particular issues of other papers. An especially
useful additional avenue of approach in this regard is the *Personal
Name Index to the New York Times Index 1851–1974*, with a *1975–
1979* supplement, which lists all names in the *Index* for the designated
years.

Bell & Howell is currently publishing indexes to a variety of U.S.
newspapers, among them the *Washington Post*, the *Chicago Tribune*,
the *Chicago Sun-Times*, the *Christian Science Monitor*, the *Los Angeles Times*, the *New Orleans Times-Picayune*, the *Detroit News*, the
Houston Post, and the *San Francisco Chronicle*. None of these, however, covers years earlier than 1972; many don't even go back that
far. Each is updated monthly, although there will be a lag of a few
months after the newspaper is out before its index appears.

Still other newspaper indexes exist in unpublished form throughout
the country in libraries, newspaper offices, and historical and genealogical societies. The best guides to these are Anita Cheek Milner's
Newspaper Indexes: A Location and Subject Guide for Researchers (3
vols.; Scarecrow, 1977–1982); Grace D. Parch's *Directory of Newspaper Libraries in the U.S. and Canada* (Special Libraries Association, 1976); and the *Lathrop Report on Newspaper Indexes* (Norman
Lathrop Enterprises, 1979–1980).

A frequent problem for researchers is that of locating a relatively
recent article when the newspaper index for the period has not yet

appeared. In these cases you should check *Facts on File,* which is a weekly news digest series. It is usually up to date to within about ten days and you can use it to find the exact dates of very recent events, which will cut down the number of newspaper issues you have to scan for the article you want. Or, if your library has computer search capabilities, for a small fee you can have a search done on a database called *Newsearch,* which covers thousands of sources including some newspapers; it is updated daily. Other computer databases contain the full text of some newspapers, updated daily (see Chapter 9).

Information Access Corporation publishes a monthly service called the *National Newspaper Index.* Like the other products of this company, this is a self-contained microfilm reader. It covers five papers, the *New York Times,* the *Christian Science Monitor,* the *Washington Post,* the *Los Angeles Times,* and the *Wall Street Journal;* each monthly microfilm is cumulative for the past three years. The system uses *Library of Congress Subject Headings,* too, which facilitates searching.

Newspapers are valuable research tools not only for the news items—their features, reviews, product evaluations, general essays on art and culture, and editorials are also most useful. Regarding the latter, some libraries subscribe to a service called *Editorials on File* that reprints full editorials—and editorial cartoons—from more than 140 U.S. and Canadian newspapers. The issues appear twice a month, and are very valuable for providing "pro and con" arguments about current issues.

Psychological and Educational Tests

One place to start looking for these is a new publication, *Tests: A Comprehensive Reference for Assessments in Psychology, Education, and Business,* edited by Richard C. Sweetland and Daniel J. Keyser (Test Corporation of America, 1986; distributed by Gale Research) and *Supplements;* this describes and evaluates over 3000 English-language tests in the designated fields and provides information on costs and availability (although no information on *reviews* of the tests). Subject access is possible through browsing the 62 categories into which the citations are arranged.

Another avenue of approach is through Oscar Buros's *Tests in Print* and his *Mental Measurements Yearbook* series. These will give you more detailed information about tests published throughout the

English-speaking world, and present critical reviews and extensive bibliographies on their use and validity. These books—like the Sweetland directory above—do not reproduce actual copies of the tests, however; for those you must usually write directly to the publisher of the test (Buros includes a directory of addresses), or try one of the other sources listed below. Buros's subject indexes also leave something to be desired, but two volumes that are easier to approach by subject are William A. Mehrens and Irving J. Lehmann's *Standardized Tests in Education* (Holt, Rinehart and Winston, 1980) and Ki-Taek Chun et al.'s *Measures for Psychological Assessment* (Survey Research Center for the Institute for Social Research, University of Michigan, 1975). These can bring to your attention tests for which you will then turn to Buros for further information.

Buros can be updated by *Psychological Abstracts;* its cumulative *Author Index* volumes for 1927–1983 are also particularly useful if you know the name of the author of the test you want. The subject heading "Tests and scales" is also valuable in both *Education Index* and *Social Sciences Index*.

To obtain an actual copy of an instrument you can always write directly to its publisher; however, there are shortcuts that sometimes work. The Educational Testing Service produces an ongoing *Tests in Microfiche* set with its own annotated index, but these are generally unpublished instruments (i.e., not the commercially available tests listed in Buros). ETS also maintains a library of tests that may be consulted on-site by serious scholars; contact Test Collection, ETS, Princeton, N.J. 08541 (1-609-921-9000) for information. A database of bibliographic information on tests in this ETS collection can be searched through the BRS computer system; ETS also sells bibliographies of tests in over two hundred subject areas. Write or call them for a free list of which bibliographies are available.

Three works by John P. Robinson et al., published by the University of Michigan's Institute for Social Research, reproduce the full text of tests: *Measures of Political Attitudes* (1968), *Measures of Social Psychological Attitudes* (rev. ed., 1973), and *Measures of Occupational Attitudes and Occupational Characteristics* (1969). Three others are also useful in this regard: Marvin E. Shaw's *Scales for the Measurement of Attitudes* (McGraw-Hill, 1967), Anita Simon and Gil Boyer's *Mirrors for Behavior III: An Anthology of Observation Instruments* (Communication Materials Center, 1974), and Gil Boyer et al.'s

Measures of Maturation: An Anthology of Early Childhood Instruments (Philadelphia: Research for Better Schools, 1973). William Goodwin and Laura A. Driscoll's *Handbook for Measurement and Evaluation in Early Childhood Education* (Jossey-Bass, 1980) presents a good explanation and overview of relevant tests. Other sources frequently very useful for researchers are doctoral dissertations—those in education and psychology often reproduce in appendices the texts of the instruments they've used. ERIC microfiche reports also occasionally include texts of instruments.

Reports

Reports are records of research findings much like journal articles, except that they have not been published in a journal and are usually available only in microfiche or reproduced-typescript formats. Copies can usually be obtained from a central clearinghouse such as the National Technical Information Service (NTIS) in Springfield, Va., or directly from their authors (whose addresses can be determined through various directories). The largest overall index to reports is the NTIS's *Government Reports Announcements & Index* (1946–   ); this is an ongoing index, with abstracts, of almost all nonclassified research reports generated by U.S. government funding or grants in all subject areas (see Chapter 12). Many other indexes to reports, however, are more comprehensive in specialized fields such as aeronautics and astronautics, agriculture, education, energy, environment, and transportation. These can be identified through Sheehy and the other sources discussed in Chapter 13. Another excellent finding aid for material in these formats is a publication available from NTIS called *How To Get It: A Guide to Defense-Related Information Sources* (see Chapter 12).

Standards and Specifications

The Library of Congress has a free four-page handout on "Major Sources of Information on Specifications and Standards"; free copies are available from the Science-Technology Reading Room (Library of Congress, Washington, D.C. 20540). It is a very good summary of a potentially confusing field, and there are only a few things to add to it:

- You can obtain free copies of any military or federal specifications by requesting them from the Naval Publications and Forms Center, 5801 Tabor Ave., Philadelphia, Pa. 19120 (1-215-697-3321). You have to know the identifying number of the standards or specs beforehand, however. If there are revisions to the specs you want, the Center is good about including them with your order, even if you haven't specifically asked for them.

- Charles Ramsay's *Architectural Graphic Standards* (Wiley, revised frequently) is useful to many people other than just architects. It provides diagrams and standard measurements of such things as tennis courts, horseshoe pits, swimming pools, door frames, fireplaces, etc.—it even diagrams the profiles of major trees, listing their average heights and spreads.

- The National Bureau of Standards in Gaithersburg, Md., maintains what is probably the world's largest collection of such material. You can write to them for information on any standard at:

  National Center for Standards and Certification Information
  Building 101, Room A633
  National Bureau of Standards
  Gaithersburg, Md. 20899

  Their telephone number is 1-301-921-2587.

- The National Standards Association mounts a computer database covering all widely used industry and government standards and specifications (ca. 100,000 citations are included); it is searchable through the Dialog system (see Chapter 9). Questions regarding the database will be answered by the organization's toll-free inquiry service at 1-800-638-8094 (Tech Info Department). The NSA will also sell you copies of standards, or provide you with information on whom to contact if they don't have the ones you want.

Statistics

The most useful compendium of statistics on all sorts of things is the federal government's annual *Statistical Abstract of the United States;* a comprehensive collection of retrospective material can be found in its companion two-volume set, *Historical Statistics of the United States,*

Colonial Times to 1970. The best indexes to statistics are from Congressional Information Service, Inc. One is *American Statistics Index* (or *ASI*, 1974–), the second is *Statistical Reference Index* (*SRI*, 1980–), and the third is *Index to International Statistics* (*IIS*, 1983–). The first is an index with abstracts of *all* statistics produced by the federal government; the second covers thousands of statistical sources from nonfederal sources (e.g., state and local governments, business, trade associations, institutes, university research centers, private polling organizations, etc.); the third includes the publications of international governmental organizations. Each contains an extremely useful Index by Categories that lists sources giving comparative data according to any of twenty geographic, economic, or demographic breakdowns (e.g., by city, state, industry, individual company, occupation, age, race, sex, etc.). Each is updated monthly with annual cumulations, and each may be accompanied by a microfiche set of the full text of the documents indexed. (The *SRI* is particularly useful for providing *rankings* of companies.)

CIS has also recently begun issuing a microfiche set of *Current National Statistical Compendiums* from 80 countries all over the world. (Note, however, that not all of these publications are in English.)

Other sources worth knowing about include the United Nations' *Statistical Yearbook, Demographic Yearbook,* and *Yearbook of International Trade Statistics,* and UNESCO's *Statistical Yearbook.* Paul Wasserman's *Statistics Sources* (Gale Research, revised irregularly) is an excellent guide to sources of data on 12,000 subjects. The *United States Department of Commerce Publications Catalog,* available from the Government Printing Office, is an inexpensive guide to many federal statistical publications, including Census reports. It also tells you how you can have customized data generated from the computer tapes of Commerce and Census. The Census Bureau also provides information over the phone on its various services, through its Data Users Services Division, Customer Services Branch, at 1-301-763-4100.

Tabular Data

The Chemical Rubber Company of Cleveland, Ohio, publishes over 50 handbooks that present tabular data in such fields as chemistry and physics, mathematics, optics, probability and statistics, microbiology, nutrition and food, and so on. The best avenue into this bewildering maze of data is the *Composite Index for CRC Handbooks* (2nd ed., CRC Press, 1977), which covers all the volumes. *Handbooks and Tables in Science and Technology* (2nd ed.; Oryx Press, 1983) is also useful.

Translations

The easiest way to find out if a foreign-language book has been translated into English is to look under the original author's name in the *National Union Catalog* and its supplements (see Chapter 10). This is likely to list most editions of the author's works in most languages; it will also tell you which libraries in North America actually own copies. The OCLC, RLIN, and WLN computer networks can perform a simmilar function. There are also various indexes that list translations of books and journal articles. The National Translations Center, now at the Library of Congress, tries to keep track of these things, and two of its publications should be consulted: *Consolidated Index of Translations into English* (1969), supplemented by the ongoing *Translations Register-Index* (1967–   ). The *World Index of Scientific Translations* (1972–   ), the National Institute of Health's *N.I.H. Library Translations Index, 1954–63* and its ongoing supplements, the annual *Index Translationum* (for which there is a cumulative index, 1948–68), and *The Literatures of the World in English Translation: A Bibliography* (3 vols.; Frederick Ungar, 1967–1970) should also be kept in mind. Bell & Howell's *Transdex* index to Joint Publications Research Service translations of foreign newspaper and journal articles, and some books, is particularly useful since all the indexed material is available in a companion microfiche set. The *Foreign Broadcast Information Service (FBIS)* translations of foreign radio broadcasts may also be useful.

Index

Where multiple page references are listed,
page numbers of the major discussion are in italics